Watching
Kansas Wildlife

Watching Kansas Wildlife

A Guide to 101 Sites

Bob Gress and George Potts

Published for the Kansas Department of Wildlife and Parks
by the University Press of Kansas

Published by the University Press of Kansas (Lawrence,
Kansas 66049), which was organized by the Kansas Board
of Regents and is operated and funded by Emporia State
University, Fort Hays State University, Kansas State
University, Pittsburg State University, the University
of Kansas, and Wichita State University

Library of Congress Cataloging-in-Publication Data

Gress, Bob.
    Watching Kansas wildlife : a guide to 101 sites / Bob
Gress and George Potts.
        p.   cm.
    Includes bibliographical references.
    ISBN 0-7006-0594-0
    1. Wildlife viewing sites—Kansas—Guidebooks
2. Wildlife watching—Kansas—Guidebooks. I. Potts,
George.   III. Kansas. Dept. of Wildlife and Parks.
III. Title.
QL 177.G73   1993
508'.09781—dc20
92-41094

Printed in Hong Kong on acid-free paper

10 9 8 7 6 5 4 3 2 1

 This book was funded by the Chickadee
Checkoff of the Kansas Department of Wildlife
and Parks. Half of the proceeds from the sale of
this book will be returned to the Chickadee Checkoff
Program to directly assist such efforts as threatened and
endangered species protection, re-introductions of sensitive wildlife, and environmental and wildlife education
programs. You can further support the wildlife you see
and enjoy from using this book through your direct
donations to Chickadee Checkoff, Kansas Department of
Wildlife and Parks, Box 54a, Route 2, Pratt KS 67124, or
by contributing on your Kansas individual income-tax
form. Do your part for wildlife conservation.

Contents

If all the beasts were gone men would die from a great loneliness of the spirit, for whatever happens to the beasts soon happens to man.—Chief Seathl (Seattle), 1854

Acknowledgments

Many people have been instrumental in the development of this guide. We especially wish to recognize Ken Brunson, the Chickadee Checkoff program coordinator for the Kansas Department of Wildlife and Parks. In addition to coordinating the funding for this project he edited the manuscript, provided wildlife expertise, site information, encouragement, and guidance. His involvement made this project a joy to work on.

Other employees of the Kansas Department of Wildlife and Parks shared their talents. Bob Mathews reviewed the manuscript. Artwork and graphics were provided by Dana Eastes. Mike Blair, Gene Brehm, Suzanne L. Collins, and Joseph T. Collins provided photographs. Rob Manes coordinated information on state public lands.

For information on sites across Kansas we would like to thank Rex Buchanan, Joseph T. Collins, Elmer Finck, Craig Freeman, Steve Harper, Jerry Hazlett, Carroll Morgenson, Galen Pittman, Stan Roth, Marvin Schwilling, Scott Seltman, Mike Watkins, and John Zimmerman.

We are also indebted to many area managers and other site coordinators who graciously provided local wildlife expertise and information for this guide.

Mike Blair

As to scenery (giving my own thought and feeling), while I know the standard claim is that Yosemite, Niagara Falls, the Upper Yellowstone, and the like afford the greatest natural shows, I am not so sure but the prairies and plains, while less stunning at first sight, last longer, fill the esthetic sense fuller, precede all the rest, and make North America's characteristic landscape.
—Walt Whitman, *Specimen Days*, 1879

Introduction

PLAINS INDIANS once fought over hunting rights to the rich wildlife grounds south of the Arkansas River valley near what is now Dodge City. Later, early explorers were amazed at the wealth of animals along the Missouri and Kansas rivers. Santa Fe Trail pioneers marveled at the great bison herds and flocks of prairie chickens. Although some of these rich natural resources have changed, Kansas still harbors a tremendous abundance and variety of wildlife. Two extraordinary wetlands endow the middle of the state: Quivira National Wildlife Refuge and Cheyenne Bottoms Wildlife Area. Cheyenne Bottoms, the state's premier wildlife-viewing area, has been formally designated as a Wetland of International Importance. Both offer excellent wildlife viewing year-round.

Kansas boasts another exceptional ecosystem the world's largest remaining tract of native tallgrass prairie. This expansive grassland, located in the scenic Flint Hills, is a source of pride to area ranchers. Their controlled fires, designed to maintain the prairie, illuminate the rolling hills with dancing beauty on warm spring nights.

Settlement of the Sunflower State in the nineteenth century brought many changes to its landscape and wildlife communities. Wolves and grizzly bears will never again roam the plains. Black-footed ferrets have disappeared from Kansas, and such other species as least terns, cave salamanders, and Neosho madtoms (a small fish) are fighting for survival. In recent times, abuses of water quality and supplies have diminished streams and wetlands. In spite of these setbacks, a few species, including white-tailed deer, bobcat, coyote, red fox, beaver, wild turkey, and Canada geese, have made astounding comebacks. Bald eagles have also done well in recent years and now winter on every major river and reservoir in the state. Many animals have adapted to our cities and rural communities and are frequently seen by alert observers.

Many amphibians and reptiles are mentioned in this book, reflecting the changing public attitude toward these less than glamorous species. Toads, frogs, lizards, salamanders, and turtles, which were always popular with kids, are numerous statewide. Snakes are becoming more appealing to adults as well. Kansas has an excellent variety of all of these warm-weather critters.

Although still rich in many wildlife resources, Kansas is not blessed with numerous public lands. Most sites are federal reservoirs or state lakes, many of which offer good wildlife-viewing opportunities. In fact, over half of the sites discussed in this book are owned by the Kansas Department of Wildlife and Parks or leased from federal agencies and managed by the department. Credit for many of these resources we all can enjoy is largely due to modern-day hunters and anglers. Their dollars and involvement have been critical to wildlife conservation and habitat maintenance in Kansas. Many of these areas have or are developing facilities for people who are physically disabled. Call ahead to obtain more specific information.

This book is not just a helpful guide. It is a celebration of the uniqueness

Bison at the Maxwell Wildlife Area are just one of the many spectacular wildlife surprises in Kansas.

of Kansas. Ponderous bison herds, white-tailed deer against a backdrop of Gypsum Hills, and prairie chickens cackling at dawn on a Flint Hills prairie are the heart of the Kansas mystique. Now the secret places of seasoned naturalists are being shared. Wherever you travel in Kansas, a wildlife-viewing area is close by. This book is designed for the novice wildlife watcher, but there is information for the experienced viewer as well. Those curious enough to investigate will find some amazing places hidden—but accessible—in the subtle hills and charming valleys of Kansas. Whether you are a Kansas citizen or a visitor to our friendly state, you will find some special wildlife treasures as you put this book to work for you and discover Kansas wildlife—America's best-kept secret!

Wildlife Viewing Tips

The best general wildlife viewing tip is the *PEQ* rule: Be *patient, early,* and *quiet.* You may need to wait several minutes, if not an hour or more, to see some wildlife species. Getting there before dawn is often necessary. Moving slowly and quietly will allow you to see wildlife spectacles you'll miss otherwise. Remember, wild animals do their best to remain hidden. Hardly anything else you do will enhance your opportunity to see and hear wildlife more than following the simple PEQ rule. Here are some more specific tips:

• Use field guides to help identify your discoveries; they may be found in most bookstores. Check with wildlife agencies for help, or consult references listed at the back of this book.

• Stop at the nearest area office or interpretive center to pick up brochures, maps, and wildlife checklists. Ask about any recent wildlife sightings.

• When visiting an area, allow plenty of time. Don't rush from one site to the next.

- Explore all the roads, trails, and habitats. Seldom are all of an area's interesting features clustered around the main entry road.

- Drive slowly, stop often, and shut off your engine to listen and look more carefully.

- Follow the PEQ rule by being in the field early but don't forget dusk. Most animals are more active at twilight than in the middle of the day.

- Use binoculars and spotting scopes to view wildlife from a distance that will not disturb them.

- Use a telephoto lens to photograph from a distance.

- Learn to interpret animal signs. Tracks, trails, nests, dens, droppings, and partially eaten plants are clues to what animals may live in the area.

- Pay close attention to "edge," the area where the prairie meets the woods or the water reaches the shore.

- After animals are spotted, don't alarm them. Talk quietly, move slowly, never directly, toward an animal. Try to stay downwind of mammals.

- If the animal is looking directly at you and appears alert and nervous, remain motionless or move slowly away until normal behavior returns.

- Stay away from animals that behave strangely or appear sickly.

- Leave pets at home. Nothing will scare animals away more quickly than a dog.

- Check with local and regional conservation groups for wildlife-viewing areas and tips. There are several Audubon chapters in Kansas and state organizations, such as the Kansas Ornithological Society, Kansas Wildflower Society, and Kansas Herpetological Society. Contact these groups to enhance your ability to find special wildlife spots and species.

- Use the Kansas Ornithological Society's Rare Bird Hotline (913-372-5499) to get an up-to-date account or to report a rare bird you have seen.

Wildlife Viewing Etiquette

People who enjoy wildlife sometimes unknowingly harm the animals. If disturbed too often, both birds and mammals may desert their nests, dens, or feeding areas. Use good judgment in viewing wildlife.

- Try to observe wildlife from a distance that will not force the animals to alter their normal behavior.

- Do not flush birds from their nests in order to view their eggs or watch them fly.

- Avoid excess use of tape players in attracting birds during their nesting season.

- Never chase wildlife.

- Limit the time you spend closely viewing an animal.

- Do not pet or rescue young animals. If the parent is not visible, it may be because you are present. Many birds and mammals leave young while feeding or during certain parts of the day.

• Leave feathers, eggs, nests, dead animals, and live animals where you find them. It is illegal to possess them without proper permits.

• After searching under rocks for reptiles or invertebrates, always replace the rocks in their original position. These small habitats take years to develop.

• Respect other viewers, recreationists, and photographers. Do not move in front of someone already in position. If an animal is approached too closely you may ruin everyone's opportunity. Don't intrude on another's area.

• Respect private property. Always get permission before entering.

• While driving on private or public lands, always stay on designated roads.

Dynamic Dozen Sites

All the sites in this guide are special. However, these top twelve sites were selected to direct you to "can't miss" opportunities. They are distinguished because of their exceptional wildlife, scenic, and viewing attributes. No matter where you are in Kansas, you are within relatively easy driving distance of at least one of these notable areas.

1. Cheyenne Bottoms Wildlife Area (Site 64)
2. Quivira National Wildlife Refuge (Site 63)
3. Gypsum Hills Wildlife Drive (Site 94)
4. Marais des Cygnes Wildlife Area (Site 25)
5. Cimarron National Grasslands (Site 101)
6. Scott State Park (Site 89)
7. Wilson Reservoir (Site 65)
8. Maxwell Wildlife Area (Site 51)
9. Chaplin Nature Center (Site 41)
10. Clinton Reservoir (Site 10)
11. Byron Walker Wildlife Area (Site 61)
12. Flint Hills Wildlife Drive (Site 47)

Dynamic Dozen Wildlife Index—Where to Go to See Popular Species

If your time or interests are limited, this index provides a quick way to find your favorites. Follow the PEQ rule (p. 2) for best results.

1. Deer—Deer can be seen at nearly every wild area site included. Many country roads along streams will offer glimpses of deer during dawn and dusk hours all during the year. Look near the edges of fields close to trees.

2. Bison (buffalo)—Sites 33, 51, 61, 89, 97, 99.

3. Wapiti (elk)—Sites 51, 73, 89, 101.

4. Pronghorns (antelope)—Sites 48, 88, 90, 91, 101.

5. Coyotes—These predators are listed in nearly half the sites but watch for them anywhere in the state. Predator calls are very effective for bringing coyotes in close.

6. Eagles—Bald eagle: Thirty-seven sites list bald eagles. Best opportunities

are the large reservoirs and river areas, along with site 11 during winter. Golden eagle: Seven sites (63, 65, 80, 84, 85, 88, 90) provide rare opportunities for golden eagles in the winter.

7. Prairie chickens—Greater prairie chicken: Sites 14, 15, 19, 20, 27, 28, 30, 44, 45, 46, 47, 48, 65, 72, 77, 82. Lesser prairie chicken: Sites 46, 93, 99, 100, 101. Best opportunities are during the April–May booming season. Check sites 46 and 101 for "reserved blind" viewing opportunities. Additional viewing blinds are being developed; contact the Kansas Department of Wildlife and Parks for updated information.

8. Wild turkeys—Thirty-four sites mention wild turkeys. Best opportunities are in early April while toms are gobbling and displaying. As with deer viewing, best sites are the many wildlife areas and managed lands around the lakes and reservoirs. Two drives, sites 47 and 94, should be rewarding during twilight and morning hours.

9. Canada Geese—Twenty-nine sites list Canada geese among many other water birds. Sure bets for seeing wintering Canada geese are the several large reservoirs, many of the listed parks, and special areas like sites 4, 25, 57, 62, 63, 64, and 84.

10. Shorebirds—There are twenty-four sites that list shorebirds, but two are absolutely "can't miss" during migrations: Quivira (6) and Cheyenne Bottoms (64). Many of the larger reservoirs also have excellent shorebird opportunities.

11. Songbirds and other birds—Nearly every site in this guide has some bird-viewing attributes. Kansas has a number of prairie-nesting species such as upland sandpipers, meadowlarks, dickcissels, and nighthawks. Beautiful neotropical birds, such as indigo and painted buntings, summer tanagers, northern parulas, and prothonotary warblers, nest at Elk City Reservoir (site 39). With over 425 species of birds, Kansas is distinguished as a prairie mecca for experienced birders and novice watchers. Places that often offer something different to the experienced birder include sites 13, 21, 25, 36, 39, 41, 63, 64, and 101.

12. Prairie dogs—Sites 63, 66, 80, 84, 85, 91, 94.

Wildlife Symbols

 Songbirds

 Water Birds

 Upland Birds

 Small Mammals

 Carnivores

 Hoofed Mammals

 Birds of Prey

 Amphibians and Reptiles

 Insects

 Wildflowers

 Fish

Recreational Symbols

$ Entry Fee	ⓐ Campground	▶ Horse Trail
P Parking	🏠 Nature Center	⊖ Canoeing
Restrooms	🚶 Nature Trail	Boat Ramp
H₂0 Drinking Water	🚶🚶 Hiking Trail	Fish Hatchery
🎔 Picnic Area	🚲 Bicycle Trail	

Site Owner/Manager Abbreviations

KDWP   Kansas Department of Wildlife and Parks
USACE   U.S. Army Corps of Engineers
USBuRec   U.S. Bureau of Reclamation
USFWS   U.S. Fish and Wildlife Service

Mike Blair

White-tailed deer, like this doe and older fawn, are most likely to be seen browsing just before dark in woodland clearings and croplands close to thickets. Bottomlands provide nearly perfect habitat for deer.

Kansas
Physiographic
Regions &
Viewing Sites

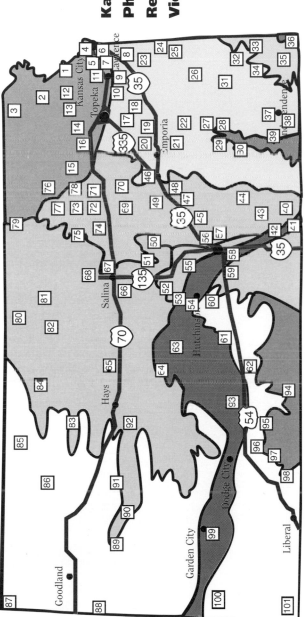

LEGEND

High Plains

Arkansas River Lowlands

Red Hills

Smoky Hills

Wellington-McPherson Lowlands

Flint Hills

Glaciated Region

Cherokee Lowlands

Osage Cuestas

Ozark Plateau

Chautauqua Hills

Wildlife Viewing Sites

northern
harrier

coyote

greater
yellow legs

muskrat

Historically the wetlands of Kansas were river overflow marshes, central basin marshes, and high plains playa lakes. These areas served as feeding stations for thousands of migrating waterfowl and as homes for many other animals. Irrigation, flood control, and

Wetlands

great blue
heron

American
avocet

raccoon

northern water
snake

painted turtle

drainage projects have reduced the number of these wetlands. Wetland reclamation programs are helping to restore some of this vital habitat.

Agricultural Lands

white-tailed
deer

badger

western
meadowlark

great plains
toad

Today the dominant feature of the Kansas landscape is agricultural land. The combination of crop fields, pastures, old farmsteads, and shelterbelts with existing streams and ponds provides food, water,

great-horned
owl

great blue
heron

coyote

rat snake

red-tailed
hawk

cover, and nesting sites for a great variety of wildlife. Our wildlife
heritage is being enriched by the many property owners throughout
the state who seek to improve habitat on their land.

Grasslands

mule deer

badger

upland
sandpiper

ornate box
turtle

western
meadowlark

Grasslands were the predominant feature of presettlement Kansas. They followed the rain—from the short and mixed grasses of the arid west to the tallgrasses of the more humid central and eastern regions of the state. The Flint Hills represent the largest remaining

red-tailed
hawk

coyote

burrowing
owl

black-tailed
prairie dog

racer

tract of tallgrass prairie in the world. Only small, isolated herds of the original thousands of bison (buffalo), pronghorn (antelope), and wapiti (American elk) that freely roamed those grasslands can now be seen.

red-bellied
woodpecker

barred owl

fox squirrel

raccoon

Early pioneers found woodlands at the eastern edge of Kansas and
along the floodplains of prairie rivers and streams. With the control
of fire by humans, woodlands have crept over lands that were origi-

Woodlands

red-tailed
hawk

white-tailed
deer

coyote

black-
and-white
warbler

rat snake

nally prairie, particularly in the eastern part of the state. As a result, some woodland animals are more abundant today than ever before.

A camera flash captured this spider lunching on a Viceroy butterfly. The prairie abounds with living beauty as well as countless life-and-death struggles.

Northeast

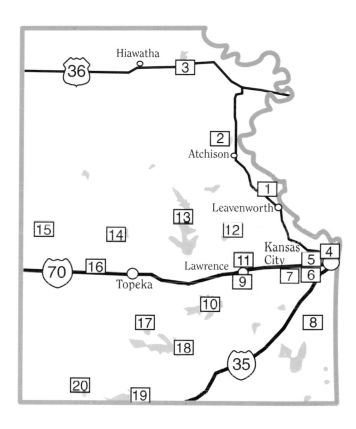

1 Weston Bend Bottomlands
2 Atchison State Fishing Lake
3 Brown State Fishing Lake
4 Wyandotte County Lake
5 Shawnee Mission Park
6 Ernie Miller Nature Center
7 The Prairie Center
8 Hillsdale Reservoir
9 Baker Wetlands and Kansas Museum of Natural History
10 Clinton Reservoir
11 Lawrence Riverfront Plaza
12 Leavenworth State Fishing Lake
13 Perry Reservoir
14 Shawnee State Fishing Lake and Wildlife Area
15 Jeffrey Energy Center
16 Green Memorial Wildlife Area
17 Osage State Fishing Lake
18 Pomona Reservoir
19 Melvern Reservoir
20 Lyon State Fishing Lake

1 Weston Bend Bottomlands

Lewis and Clark watched wildlife here! Weston Bend, alongside the Missouri River below the limestone bluffs that anchor Fort Leavenworth, is one of the best examples of riparian bottomlands in Kansas. Before the construction of dikes, jetties, and levees, the Missouri meandered between the east and west bluffs, leaving oxbow lakes and depositing enough fertile soil to produce a paradise of plants and animals. A network of trails from the main levee takes you through woodlands, old croplands, and marshes and along sloughs and ponds. In the mature woodlands of cottonwood, sycamore, hackberry, and walnut, listen for pileated woodpeckers hammering holes in dead trees. The tops of some sycamores hold four-feet-wide stick nests of great blue herons. The young riparian woodlands contain immature cottonwood, elm, and ash, as well as elderberries and raspberries. The tender cottonwood shoots and branches provide great browsing for white-tailed deer and beaver. The birdlife of Weston Bend is notable. Towhees, chickadees, woodpeckers, grosbeaks, buntings, warblers, orioles, and vireos are abundant during migrations. Spring rains can turn the bottomlands into an attractive wetland, harboring thousands of migrating waterfowl. Coyotes, foxes, and raccoons take advantage of the bounty.

Directions: In Leavenworth, take Metropolitan Avenue (U.S. 73) to the entrance of Fort Leavenworth at 7th Street. Take Grant for about 1.5 miles to the Disciplinary Barracks. To the right of the barracks is Riverside Drive. Take it about 0.2 mile to Chief Joseph Loop. Cross the railroad tracks and go just past the picnic grounds. The loop, which becomes the levee road from which the trails are found, is one way and will lead you back to Riverside Drive. For information, write Forestry Department, Directorate of Engineering and Housing, Bldg. 85, Fort Leavenworth KS 66027. **Ownership:** U.S. Army (913-684-2749) **5,600 acres** 🅿 🏕

2 Atchison State Fishing Lake

Atchison State Fishing Lake is nestled among rounded hills blanketed by oak-hickory woodlands and broad valleys planted in corn. The 2.5 miles of gravel road from K-7 to the Independence Creek valley, where the lake is located, are like a roller coaster and can be slick when wet. Elm, willow, silver maple, and locust compose the riparian woodland, where wildflowers are abundant from spring through fall. Butterflies are commonly seen in the woodlands and along the lake edge during the summer. Both fox and gray squirrels scamper through the trees. Tracks of white-tailed deer and raccoons cover the banks of the creek and lake. Red-eyed and yellow-throated vireos, blue-gray gnatcatchers, and summer tanagers nest here. Summer evenings bring the clear, mellow song of the whip-poor-will and the loud whistling call of the chuck-will's-widow. During fall and spring migrations, the lake will host puddle ducks (such as mallards and pintails) and diving ducks, including goldeneyes and redheads. Shorebirds are also present during migrations.

Directions: From Atchison go 3 miles north on K-7. Take the gravel road 2 miles west and 0.5 miles north to the lake. **Ownership:** KDWP (913-246-3449) **248 acres** 🅿 ⚇ H_2O 🏕 🌀

3 Brown State Fishing Lake

Brown State Fishing Lake is set in the Glaciated Region. Surrounding fields of winter wheat and corn stubble help feed thousands of snow geese from November through January. Controlled burning of the native bluestem prairie helps optimize the balance of brush and grass necessary for bob-white quail and ring-necked pheasant. Post-burn wildflowers are spectacular, as are the butterflies they attract. Signs of beaver and muskrat can be found around the lake and the three streams feeding it. In spring and fall, waterfowl and shorebirds are common on the lake and on the mudflats of shallow coves. Migrant songbirds are numerous. Tracks of white-tailed deer, bobcats, mink, skunks, and opossums can be found in the mud along the shores.

Directions: Travel 9 miles east of Hiawatha on U.S. 36. Turn north, then immediately turn west, and drive 0.8 miles to the lake. **Ownership:** KDWP (913-246-3449) **189 acres**

4 Wyandotte County Lake

Just northwest of Kansas City, Kansas, in a setting of hillside oak-hickory woodlands and lakeside sycamores, is Wyandotte County Lake. Stop first at the Administration Building (where you will be accosted by Canada geese seeking a handout) and pick up a map and checklist. Best viewing sites for water birds are the south side, west lookout, Boathouse Cove, and Wilson Cove. There are many pullouts for viewing woodland wildlife. During spring and fall migrations, search the lake for northern shovelers, northern pintails, green-winged teal, blue-winged teal, common goldeneyes, buffle-heads, common mergansers, and hooded mergansers. On occasion, an osprey will be fishing the lake. Survey the woodlands for migrating warblers and vireos. In winter, bald eagles and rough-legged hawks may visit. On warm summer nights listen for the calls of eastern screech-owls, great horned owls, and whip-poor-wills. Early daylight and dusk are the best times to watch for wading herons, wild turkeys, white-tailed deer, beaver, opossums, raccoons, and foxes.

Directions: From I-70 take I-435 north to Leavenworth Road (Exit 15). Travel east 1.7 miles to 91st Street, then 0.6 miles north to the Administration Building. **Ownership:** Wyandotte County Park (913-299-0550) **1,900 acres**

Deer and wild turkey are plentiful statewide and are featured in most of the sites listed.

5 Shawnee Mission Park

Here's some urban wildlife you won't want to miss! Located at 7900 Renner Road in Shawnee, Shawnee Mission Park is the largest of the Johnson County parks. This 1,250-acre urban refuge includes a 150-acre lake, ponds, marshes, thickets, and meadows. On the west boundary, experience the Mill Creek Streamway Trail. This meandering 8-mile asphalt treadway takes you along the stream and through riparian and hillside oak-hickory forests and upland native prairies. White-tailed deer, gray and fox squirrels, red and gray foxes, and wild turkeys are sometimes sighted by hikers. Northern cardinals, black-capped chickadees, tufted titmice, downy and red-bellied woodpeckers are commonly seen. On spring evenings listen for the call of the whip-poor-will. In the spring and fall check the lake and ponds for pied-billed grebes and mallard ducks. Ospreys occasionally fish the lake. Don't overlook the common snipe and spotted sandpipers on the shoreline. The marshy ponds below the dam attract red-winged blackbirds, belted kingfishers, and great blue herons. In winter you may see a bald eagle perched on a shoreline tree.

Directions: From I-35 take westbound I-435 to 87th Street Parkway. Travel west to Renner Road, then north to the park entrance and interpretive center at 79th Street. **Ownership:** Johnson County Parks & Recreation (913-831-3355) **1,250 acres** P ⛹ H₂0 ⛱ ⛺ ⚐ ⚐

The opossum is the only marsupial found in North America. The mother carries her young in her pouch for the first 11 weeks, they ride piggyback for the next 3 weeks, and then they're on their own.

Bob Gress

Mike Blair

The clear whistle of the male northern cardinal declares his presence in the spring. Seen along woodland edges and streamside thickets throughout the state, this red-crested "noble" and his mate can be drawn to your backyard by planting trees and shrubs and filling feeders with black oil sunflower seeds.

6 Ernie Miller Nature Center

A beautiful, relaxing spot, the Ernie Miller Nature Center, on the west edge of Olathe, was created to heighten awareness of the natural world. Nature and walking trails meander along streams and through riparian and oak-hickory woodlands and native prairie. The education building features exhibits, a gift shop, and a bird-feeder court with butterfly and hummingbird gardens. Big and little bluestem, switchgrass, Indiangrass, and numerous species of wildflowers are found in the prairie. The woodlands include American elm, hackberry, black walnut, bur oak, bittersweet, sumac, and buckbrush. Mammals sighted year-round are white-tailed deer, eastern cottontail rabbits, woodchucks, raccoons, gray squirrels, and fox squirrels. In summer, five-lined skinks and slender glass lizards can be seen scampering and slithering through woodland debris. Many species of sparrows and warblers migrate through the area in the spring and fall. Nesting varieties include warblers, vireos, thrushes, thrashers, swifts, and swallows. Rough-legged hawks are frequently observed in the winter, as are black-capped chickadees, tufted titmice, American goldfinches, and dark-eyed juncos.

Directions: From I-35 travel west on K-150 through Olathe to K-7. Travel north about 1.5 miles. The entrance is on the west side of K-7. **Ownership:** Johnson County Parks & Recreation (913-831-3355) **113 acres**

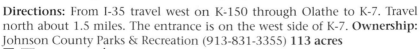

The large black swallowtail is one of 182 species of butterflies in Kansas. It can be seen dashing a few feet above the ground over prairies, gardens, streamsides, and roadsides throughout the state from mid-April through October.

Mike Blair

7 The Prairie Center

The Prairie Center, just west of Olathe, showcases the tallgrass prairie of Kansas with self-guided nature trails. Mid-April burning helps maintain tallgrasses, including big and little bluestem, switchgrass, and Indiangrass. The burn also enhances wildflowers. Look for blossoming spiderwort, Carolina anemone, and wild strawberry in the spring. In late May or early June, the endangered Meade's milkweed blooms here. Prickly poppy, Illinois bundleflower, and sensitive brier (whose leaves fold when they are touched) flower in summer. Blooming in fall are smooth aster, downy gentian, and Missouri goldenrod. A variety of butterflies can be seen around the wildflowers. Prairie birds that inhabit the area include eastern meadowlarks, grasshopper sparrows, American kestrels, mourning doves, and common nighthawks. Look for slender glass lizards, ringneck snakes, ornate box turtles, and other reptiles in the early summer. Mammals include white-tailed deer and coyotes. Prominent geological features are the limestone bluffs along the west branch of Cedar Creek and quartzite boulders left by ice-age glaciers.

Directions: From the intersection of I-35 and K-150 in Olathe, travel 6 miles west to the corner of 135th Street and Prairie Center Road. **Ownership:** KDWP (913-783-4507) **293 acres**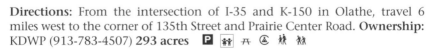

8 Hillsdale Reservoir

Travelers to Hillsdale Reservoir should stop at the visitor center at the northeast end of the dam. Many interpretive displays explain the lake's history, recreational opportunities, and natural resources. (If you are planning to visit the western parts of the lake, be sure to pick up a map because the roads can be confusing.) Behind the center, bird feeders attract resident sparrows, juncos, woodpeckers, and chickadees. The 0.75-mile Hidden Spring Nature Trail, which begins at the visitor center, takes hikers through an oak-hickory forest. Look for fox squirrels, white-tailed deer, woodland birds, and a couple of the most respected reptiles in eastern Kansas: the venomous timber rattlesnake and the copperhead. Flocks of ducks, geese, pelicans, and gulls are seen on the lake during migrations. Late November may bring large flocks of snow geese. At the bridge over Little Bull Creek, scan the flooded timber for wintering bald eagles. Throughout the year, look for cormorants, gulls, grebes, and ducks. A great blue heron nesting colony is visible to the west from the Rock Creek bridge. With binoculars and a spotting scope, approximately 50 large stick nests can be seen in the tallest sycamores growing from the creek bottom about 0.5 miles away.

Directions: From the intersection of U.S. 169 and K-68, north of Paola, drive 3 miles north to 255th Street. The Hillsdale Reservoir Visitor Center lies 3.2 miles west of this intersection through the town of Hillsdale. **Ownership:** USACE (913-783-4366); KDWP (913-783-4507) **13,100 acres**

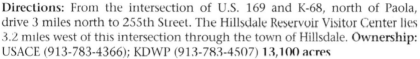

9 Baker Wetlands and Kansas Museum of Natural History

Baker Wetlands, which has been designated by the National Park Service as a National Natural Landmark, is important habitat for the sensitive northern crawfish frog. Located just south of Lawrence, Baker Wetlands is part of the Wakarusa River bottomlands. The north half of the site is wetland. The south part consists of riparian woodland, old cropland, and two plots of native prairie totaling 45 acres. The prairie areas contain prairie cordgrass, eastern gamagrass, switchgrass, Indiangrass, big bluestem, swamp milkweed, compass plant, Jerusalem artichoke, and Maximilian sunflower. Smallmouth salamanders breed here in March. Other amphibians include western chorus frogs and leopard frogs. Many times the area is dry, but when water is plentiful, so are the rails, ducks, shorebirds, and herons. Songbirds include marsh wrens, sedge wrens, swamp sparrows, LeConte's sparrows, and common yellowthroats. When you are in Lawrence, you should visit the Kansas Museum of Natural History located in Dyche Hall on the campus of the University of Kansas. The museum offers a number of interesting educational displays about natural sites in Kansas, as well as a gift shop.

Directions: Baker Wetlands is just south of the Lawrence city limits on 31st Street between Haskell and Louisiana streets. Park and walk in from the north gate, halfway between Haskell and Louisiana, or from the east gate at 35th and Haskell. **Ownership:** Baker University (913-594-3172); University of Kansas (913-864-4180) **573 acres**

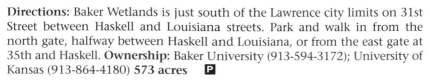

10 Clinton Reservoir

Home of the bald eagle! In 1989 Clinton Reservoir generated statewide headlines when a pair of bald eagles nested in the Deer Creek arm of the reservoir. This was the first nesting in Kansas since pioneer days. The birds have returned annually to the highly protected aerie. High limestone bluffs, clear water, wooded shorelines, tallgrass prairie, croplands, and miles of hiking and camping trails make this one of the most remarkable recreation and wildlife-viewing sites in Kansas. Start your visit at the Corps of Engineers Information Center. A walk on the Backwoods Nature Trail will give you the opportunity to learn about the natural history of this area. Visit the dam and its overlook on the north end, drive through the Clinton Wildlife Area in the upper reaches of the reservoir, and walk the various hiking trails. The prairie blooms from spring to fall with prairie violets, Missouri evening primrose, lead plant, butterfly milkweed, Baldwin ironweed, and dozens of other wildflowers. Bullfrogs and painted turtles are found in the wetlands in summer. Look for slender glass lizards along the bluebird trail. Squirrels, foxes, coyotes, white-tailed deer, bobcats, beaver, and mink are sighted year-round. Nesting birds include Canada geese, wood ducks, red-bellied woodpeckers, rose-breasted grosbeaks, mourning doves, eastern bluebirds, red-tailed hawks, and American kestrels.

Directions: To reach the dam, travel 3 miles west of Lawrence on U.S. 40 to County Road 13, then 2 miles south. Maps, hiking and horse trail information, and Backwoods Nature Trail guides are available in the Corps of Engineers Information Center, just north of the dam. Park permits, camping information, and the wildlife area map can be obtained from the Clinton State Park office, about 1 mile west of the Corps center. **Ownership:** USACE (913-843-7665); KDWP (913-842-8562) **18,856 acres**

$ P 👫 H₂0 ⇟ Ⓐ 🚶 🚶🚶 ▶ 🚫 ⇌

The shy, mild-mannered timber rattlesnake can become testy when walked on, so look over rocks and logs before you step. Timber rattlers are found on rocky hillsides in the eastern third of Kansas.

Suzanne L. Collins & Joseph T. Collins

Pushed close to extinction, the bald eagle has made an astounding comeback since the banning of DDT in 1972. Now this beautiful bird of prey is a common winter resident at most large reservoirs and rivers in Kansas and has recently successfully nested at two sites in the state.

11 Lawrence Riverfront Plaza

Shopping for eagles? A visit to the Lawrence Riverfront Plaza from November through March offers unique close-up views of wintering bald eagles. The plaza is located on the south bank of the Kansas River in downtown Lawrence. Through large windows on the north side of the mall you can see eagles feeding below the Bowersock Dam waterfall and perching on riverbank cottonwood trees as close as 20 feet. The Bowersock Mill and Power Plant above the dam diverts, warms, then returns the river water, making it free of ice, even in the coldest winters. When area reservoirs freeze in January and February, the site below the dam is often the only open water in the region and frequently attracts as many as 40 bald eagles. There are usually a half dozen or more eagles at the plaza during the winter. The best time to view them is early in the day. Because of the bald eagles, special conditions were set for the construction and management of the plaza, including restricted use of the promenade during winter. With impact to eagles minimized, there is a tremendous educational and viewing opportunity within a comfortable controlled winter climate.

Directions: The Lawrence Riverfront Plaza is located at 6th and Massachusetts in downtown Lawrence. **Ownership:** Lawrence Riverfront Plaza (913-842-5511)   **P**

12 Leavenworth State Fishing Lake

Leavenworth State Fishing Lake in the Glaciated Region is surrounded by tallgrass prairie, oak-hickory forest, and riparian woodland. On the hillsides are bur, chinquapin, white, red, and black oaks, plus bitternut and shagbark hickory. Willow, elm, locust, box elder, and silver maple line the lakeshore. The uplands are native bluestem prairie. This forest-prairie mosaic, along with the lake and wetlands, supports a multitude of wildlife. As you approach the lake, survey the grasslands for prairie birds. In fall and spring scan the open waters for common goldeneyes, buffleheads, canvasbacks, mallards, northern pintails, and northern shovelers. In winter, many geese use this lake. Blue-gray gnatcatchers, yellow-throated vireos, Kentucky warblers, yellow warblers, and northern orioles nest in the area. Listen at night for chuck-will's-widows, whip-poor-wills, barred owls, and great horned owls. In the dim light of dusk and dawn, white-tailed deer, wild turkeys, opossums, raccoons, and beaver are active. By mid-morning gray and fox squirrels can be seen scampering through the trees.

Directions: From Tonganoxie, go 3 miles north on K-90; then take the blacktop 2 miles west. **Ownership:** KDWP (913-842-8562) **940 acres**

Gene Brehm

In April and May the gobbling of this male wild turkey can be heard a mile away. Large flocks of these permanent Kansas residents can be seen foraging for acorns, seeds, and nuts at riparian woodland sites throughout the state.

13 Perry Reservoir

Perry Reservoir is in the beautiful Delaware River valley of the Glaciated Region. The rolling bluestem prairie and hillsides of oak and hickory yield a large variety of wildlife. The reservoir, meadows, old fields, and riparian woodlands, as well as the marshes and mudflats, furnish living space for additional species. Hike on the Perry Reservoir National Recreation Trail through the shoreline and hillside communities. Visit Perry Wildlife Area to view the shallow-water habitats of the upper reservoir. In spring and early summer, search the mudflats for shorebirds. Among the cattails and sedges of the marsh you may find nesting sedge wrens, ducks, herons, muskrats, beaver, and mink. Watch for wild turkeys, pileated woodpeckers, rose-breasted grosbeaks, and white-tailed deer in the riparian woodlands. American kestrels, eastern meadowlarks, horned larks, and coyotes can be observed in the old fields and meadows. The oak-hickory ridges attract buntings, vireos, tanagers, thrushes, and warblers. Gulls, pelicans, ducks, and flocks of snow geese are common on the open waters during the fall migration. In winter bald eagles perch in tall trees at the water's edge.

Directions: From U.S. 24 at Perry, travel 3 miles north to the Corps of Engineers Information Center (maps and trail information are available). The Perry Reservoir State Park Office is 5 miles west of Perry on U.S. 24, then 5 miles north on K-237. The office has park permits and maps of the wildlife area. **Ownership:** USACE (913-597-5144); KDWP (913-246-3449) **22,134 acres**

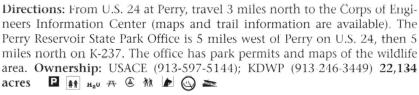

14 Shawnee State Fishing Lake and Wildlife Area

Shawnee State Fishing Lake and Wildlife Area lies in the Glaciated Region a few miles northwest of Topeka. The surrounding landscape is characterized by big and little bluestem, Indiangrass, switchgrass, and a profusion of prairie animals. Songbirds, such as eastern meadowlarks, dickcissels, and grasshopper sparrows, can be heard and seen. Red-tailed hawks, mourning doves, ring-necked pheasants, and greater prairie chickens are common. In late spring listen for western chorus frogs. Reptiles include ornate box turtles and six-lined racerunners. Sliders and painted turtles are often observed sunning on water snags on summer days. Great blue herons, beaver, and muskrats can be viewed around the reservoir. Eastern cottontails and white-tailed deer are also common. Of geological interest are pink quartzite rocks that were plowed up in South Dakota and carried to Kansas by huge glaciers.

Directions: Take U.S. 75 north of Topeka to 62nd Street. Travel 3 miles west to Landon Road, 2 miles north to 86th Street, then 1.2 miles west to the lake. **Ownership:** KDWP (913-246-3449) **640 acres**

Fondly called the "prairie canary," this delightful American goldfinch is a year-round resident. These colorful birds can be seen in weed patches, open second-growth woodlands, and roadside ditches containing thistles and sunflowers through-out most of Kansas.

Mike Blair

15 Jeffrey Energy Center

Recharge your batteries! The Jeffrey Energy Center is a large coal-powered electricity-generating plant north of St. Mary's. Public access is monitored 24 hours daily at the main entry gate. Three lakes and three wildlife management areas provide excellent wildlife watching. Commonly seen on the lakes during migrations are geese, ducks, common mergansers, and double-crested cormorants. Herons, kingfishers, plovers, sandpipers, and gulls are common in the shallows and along the shorelines. On occasion ospreys are seen fishing the lakes. In late fall, bald eagles are present. Large numbers of snow geese winter here. From March through November look in the grass-lands for upland sandpipers, eastern meadowlarks, dickcissels, mourning doves, and grasshopper sparrows. Watch also for red-tailed hawks, northern harriers, and American kestrels. Booming grounds of greater prairie chickens can be found west of Make-Up Lake. Quail, wild turkeys, white-tailed deer, raccoons, and coyotes are common. On rare occasions a bobcat is seen. The rocky areas are good places to find fossils and reptiles.

Directions: From U.S. 24 at St. Mary's, travel 5 miles north on K-63, then 3.3 miles west to the entry gate. Pick up an area map, nature trail guide, and other information here. **Ownership:** Western Resources, Inc. (913-456-2035; 913-575-6310) **10,265 acres** P 🚻 ⛟ 🚶 ♿ 🛶

16 Green Memorial Wildlife Area

Quaint and colorful! An oak-hickory-bluestem mix at the southern edge of the Glaciated Region is the small, quiet, natural setting for the Green Memorial Wildlife Area. Restored bluestem prairie, oak-hickory hillsides, and a bubbly brook are the intermingling habitats at this site. Hike the Post Creek Ridge and Oregon Trace nature trails. The pink quartzite rock was transported from South Dakota by glaciers during the Kansan Ice Age. Shingle oak, red oak, redbud, pawpaw, and western buckeye make up the woodlands. Spring through fall, wildflowers such as ox-eye daisy, coneflowers, compass plant, penstemon, black sampson, and black-eyed Susan are seen in the prairie plots. Wildlife food is provided by wild gooseberry, elderberry, black raspberry, highbush blackberry, wild strawberry, and riverbank and raccoon grape. Look for five-lined skinks, racers, and ornate box turtles. Cricket frogs frequently call on spring and summer nights. The nests of eastern woodrats can be found in rock crevices. Signs of coyotes, raccoons, red foxes, and white-tailed deer are abundant. Great horned owls, downy and red-bellied woodpeckers, cardinals, blue jays, vireos, and warblers are found in the woods. Upland sandpipers, eastern meadowlarks, scissor tailed flycatchers, eastern kingbirds, red-tailed hawks, American kestrels, and northern harriers can be seen in the grasslands.

Directions: Take I-70 10 miles west of Topeka to the Rossville turnoff. Go 2.5 miles north to Willard. Take 2nd Street 0.5 miles east to Gilkerson Street. Follow Gilkerson 0.7 miles south to the wildlife area. **Ownership:** KDWP (913-246-3449) **83 acres** 🅿 🚶

17 Osage State Fishing Lake

Osage State Fishing Lake lies in a small, pleasant valley of the Osage Cuestas. Around the lake is a riparian woodland, and the upland is native bluestem prairie. In fall and spring the water attracts migrating waterfowl including snow geese, Canada geese, mallards, pintails, common mergansers, and common goldeneyes. On occasion a migrating osprey is seen plunging, talons first, into the lake for fish. Eastern screech-owls, great horned owls, northern flickers, hairy woodpeckers, eastern wood-pewees, and white-breasted nuthatches can be found in the woods. In summer search the fields and prairies for eastern meadowlarks, mourning doves, northern bobwhite quail, grasshopper sparrows, scissor-tailed flycatchers, and both eastern and western kingbirds. In the nesting season listen for the boom of diving male nighthawks courting their mates. Common around the lake are muskrats and beavers. Watch for white-tailed deer and coyotes year-round.

Directions: Take U.S. 75 3.5 miles south of Carbondale and 0.7 miles east to the lake. **Ownership:** KDWP (913-828-4933) **506 acres** 🅿 🚻 H₂O 🍽 ⊘ ⚓

Bob Gress

Raccoon tracks are commonly seen in the mud along streams and ponds. These nocturnal mammals eat a variety of small animals and are excellent swimmers.

18 Pomona Reservoir

Pomona Reservoir is on 110 Mile Creek, just a few miles above its confluence with the Marais des Cygnes River. Here, in the Osage Cuestas, the tallgrass prairie adjoins valleys of black and chinquapin oak, and shagbark and bitternut hickory. To become familiar with area plants and animals, walk Witches' Broom Nature Trail in the Army Corps of Engineers park and the nature trail in the state park. Cottonwood, hackberry, and American elm are common in the riparian timber. Thickets of aromatic sumac, smooth sumac, and rough-leaved dogwood provide good cover for many species of wildlife. More than 4,000 acres are managed for wildlife. Plantings for food and cover include native grasses, alternating weed strips, and standing crops. Spend some time at the state park office viewing the bird feeder through the big window. Bird visitors include red-bellied woodpeckers, white-breasted nuthatches, black-capped chickadees, purple finches, and Carolina wrens. In winter you can see bald eagles perched on tall lakeshore trees and rough-legged hawks over the prairie. Throughout migrations you can expect to see snow and Canada geese, buffleheads, goldeneyes, mergansers, mallards, teal, wigeons, pintails, and pelicans. In the mudflats there are killdeer, dowitchers, and yellowlegs. Watch the woodlands for squirrels along with warblers, vireos, and buntings. White-tailed deer, eastern cottontails, eastern woodrats, raccoons, opossums, bobcats, and coyotes are also present.

Directions: To reach the Pomona State Park office, travel 2 miles north from Lyndon on U.S. 75 to K-268. Follow K-268 6 miles east and 1 mile north. The Corps of Engineers Information Center is 2 miles east of the state park office on the northeast side of the dam. Maps and trail guides are available at both offices. Park permits can be purchased at the state park office. **Ownership:** USACE (913-453-2202); KDWP (913-828-4933) **10,500 acres**

19 Melvern Reservoir

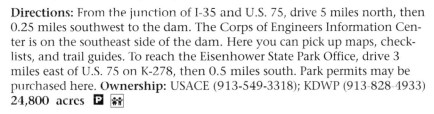

It cut through gently rolling hills of tallgrass, and its marshes teemed with waterfowl and other wildlife. It is the river the French trappers named the Marais des Cygnes (Marsh of the Swans). Melvern Reservoir, in the valley of that river, is still a haven for many of the wildlife species seen by the early trappers. A good way to become familiar with the area is to walk on the Marais des Cygnes Nature Trail below the dam and on the Eisenhower Nature Trail in Eisenhower State Park. There are riparian woodlands of ash, American elm, cottonwood, and honey locust, and thickets of rough-leaved dogwood, smooth sumac, and wild plum. Hundreds of acres of big and little bluestem, Indiangrass, switchgrass, black sampson, black-eyed Susan, Illinois bundleflower, and dozens of other prairie plants are found here. The river, lake, and cattail marshes provide habitat for many migrating waterfowl, shorebirds, and wading birds. In winter bald eagles perch in trees along the lake. Also watch for sharp-shinned, Cooper's, and rough-legged hawks. The waters attract snow geese, gadwalls, American wigeons, and common mergansers. Look in the woodlands and thickets for black-capped chickadees, red-breasted nuthatches, tufted titmice, and brown creepers. In spring, grasslands contain booming grounds, or leks, of greater prairie chickens. Summer birds include wood ducks, scissor-tailed flycatchers, eastern kingbirds, common nighthawks, and great blue herons. Year-round residents include red-tailed hawks, northern harriers, eastern screech-owls, Canada geese, belted kingfishers, and red headed woodpeckers. Mammals such as white-tailed deer, squirrels, bobcats, coyotes, muskrats, and beaver can best be viewed just before sunup and just after sundown.

Directions: From the junction of I-35 and U.S. 75, drive 5 miles north, then 0.25 miles southwest to the dam. The Corps of Engineers Information Center is on the southeast side of the dam. Here you can pick up maps, checklists, and trail guides. To reach the Eisenhower State Park Office, drive 3 miles east of U.S. 75 on K-278, then 0.5 miles south. Park permits may be purchased here. **Ownership:** USACE (913-549-3318); KDWP (913-828-4933) **24,800 acres** 🅿 🚻

20 Lyon State Fishing Lake

This lake is in the tallgrass prairie but much of it is bordered by red cedar, rough-leaved dogwood, smooth sumac, hackberry, and elm. Meadowlarks, mourning doves, Bell's vireos, rufous-sided towhees, and bobwhite quail nest here. In the spring, you can locate booming grounds of the greater prairie chicken by driving along the roads at sunrise and listening carefully for the "cackling" and "cooing" sounds. During migrations the lake attracts ducks and geese and several species of songbirds, including Harris' sparrows, cardinals, robins, and tree sparrows. Long-eared owls sometimes roost in the cedar trees during winter. In the woodlands, watch for white-tailed deer, fox squirrels, and the nests of eastern wood rats. These large, domed, stick nests built around the base of a tree, or sometimes several feet off the ground, are quite visible. To birders, the area is probably best known as a place to find Smith's longspurs. To find these birds, be prepared for a challenge and walk the mowed hayfields on the south side of the lake. Watch for small flocks of buff-colored birds about the size of sparrows with a white shoulder patch and white outer tail feathers. During summer these birds return to the high arctic to nest.

Directions: From the intersection of I-35 and K-99, on the north edge of Emporia, travel north on K-99 for 13 miles. Follow the sign east for 2 miles to the lake entrance. **Ownership:** KDWP (913-828-4933) **582 acres**

Buffalo and elk may be seen at a number of managed facilities around Kansas.

Southeast

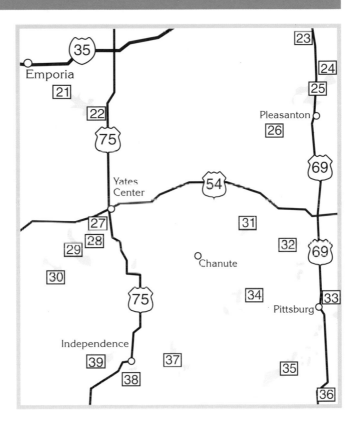

21 Flint Hills National
   Wildlife Refuge

22 John Redmond Reservoir

23 Miami State Fishing Lake
   and Wildlife Area

24 La Cygne Lake and Wildlife Area

25 Marais des Cygnes Wildlife Area

26 Dingus Natural Area

27 Yates Center Reservoir

28 Woodson State Fishing Lake
   and Wildlife Area

29 Toronto Reservoir

30 Fall River Reservoir

31 Bourbon State Fishing Lake
   and Wildlife Area

32 Crawford State Fishing Lake

33 Mined Land Wildlife Area No. 1

34 Neosho Wildlife Area

35 Mined Land Wildlife Area Nos.
   20 to 23

36 Schermerhorn Park

37 Big Hill Reservoir

38 Montgomery State Fishing Lake

39 Elk City Reservoir

21 Flint Hills National Wildlife Refuge

Flint Hills National Wildlife Refuge—a place of great variety—is on the Neosho River at the upper end of John Redmond Reservoir. This large waterfowl management area, which is in the western portion of the Osage Cuestas, is noted for its diverse habitats: wetlands, croplands, old fields, and tallgrass prairie. It is home—at one time of the year or another—to 7 species of woodpeckers, 13 species of flycatchers, 25 species of sparrows, and 31 species of warblers. Turkey vultures float the thermals on summer days and fireflies illuminate summer nights. Thousands of Mexico-bound monarch butterflies migrate through in September. Up to 150 bald eagles and more than 100,000 snow geese may spend the winter here. Foxes, coyotes, bobcats, bobwhite quail, wild turkeys, woodchucks, raccoons, and many other species hunt and forage year-round. The threatened Neosho madtom, a small fish, haunts the gravel bars in the Neosho River that winds through the refuge. Spiderwort, ragwort, and phlox bloom in spring. Sunflowers and silphium flower in summer, and goldenrods and asters blossom in fall. In summer, upland sandpipers, dickcissels, grasshopper sparrows, and eastern meadowlarks are commonly seen singing from fenceposts. At Goose Bend Marsh watch for waders such as great blue and green-backed herons feeding on fish and leopard frogs. Look also for ducks, muskrats, and several species of water snakes. The Dove Roost Pond Trail is a good spot for songbirds, fox squirrels, white-tailed deer, and cottontail rabbits.

Directions: From the I-35 and the K-130 turnoff (Exit 141), travel 8 miles south to Flint Hills National Wildlife Refuge Headquarters at Hartford. Checklists, maps, and brochures are available. **Ownership:** U.S. Fish and Wildlife Service (316-392-5553) **18,463 acres** ▣ 👫 H₂0 ⊼ Ⓒ ⛰ 🚶 ⊘ ⇌

22 John Redmond Reservoir

John Redmond Reservoir spans the broad floodplain of the Neosho River near the town of New Strawn. Located in the Central Flyway, Redmond is an important stopover for many species of migrating waterfowl. The nearby croplands of wheat, corn, and milo provide food for the migrating birds. During migrations greater and lesser yellowlegs, long-billed dowitchers, and other shorebirds are found in the mudflats. The surrounding bluestem pastures support many grassland animals. Otter Creek Wildlife Area is managed to maintain ample food, cover, and breeding areas for wildlife. In winter bald eagles perch in trees near the dam, and rough-legged hawks float overhead. Thousands of snow geese are in the area during the winter. Year-round, white-tailed deer, bobwhite quail, cottontail rabbits, raccoons, opossums, and coyotes can be seen in the Otter Creek area. In summer, look in the shallow waters for great blue and green-backed herons. Be sure to visit the 18,500-acre Flint Hills National Wildlife Refuge at the northern end of the lake.

Directions: To reach the dam, take U.S. 75 to the south end of New Strawn. Turn west, then follow the Redmond road southwest, a little over 1 mile. Maps and other information are available at the Corps of Engineers Information Center northeast of the dam. **Ownership:** USACE (316-364-8614); KDWP (913-828-4933) **10,870 acres**

▣ 👫 H₂0 ⊼ Ⓒ 🚶 ⊘ ⇌

23 Miami State Fishing Lake and Wildlife Area

When approaching this area, visitors travel through wooded farm country with some remnants of tallgrass prairie. White-tailed deer thrive in this habitat. Loggerhead shrikes, American kestrels, and eastern meadowlarks are common. The lake lies in a scenic valley along the Marais des Cygnes River. The access road travels between the lake and the steep riverbank. Hills and trees provide a protected retreat for anglers as well as migrating waterfowl. Ducks, grebes, and mergansers stop here, as well as wintering bald eagles, which are easily observed against the hillsides bordering the east side of the lake. Woodland areas are very attractive in spring and fall for migrating songbirds. The roadway provides walking access for those searching for warblers, tanagers, vireos, flycatchers, and orioles. Woodpeckers and owls are also residents of the wooded riverbanks. Copperheads may be found here.

Directions: From La Cygne, follow the signs approximately 6 miles north to the lake entrance. **Ownership:** KDWP (913-783-4507) **267 acres**

These young eastern screech-owls recently left the security of their tree cavity nest. Only eight inches tall, these raptors feed on a wide assortment of insects and small mammals.

> *Thousands of snow geese stop at Flint Hills National Wildlife Refuge during the winter.*

24 La Cygne Lake and Wildlife Area

La Cygne Lake was created to cool the coal-fired electricity-generating plant at the east end of the dam. Bald eagles and waterfowl are attracted to the lake during migrations and through the winter. Look for a variety of ducks as well as double-crested cormorants, eared and horned grebes, and common mergansers. Great blue herons, green-backed herons, and belted kingfishers are attracted to the water's edge. On the western shore of the lake is Linn County Park; oak-hickory woodlands attract warblers, vireos, tanagers, and flycatchers during the spring migration. In the evenings listen for barred owls, eastern screech-owls, whip-poor-wills, and chuck-will's-widows. In the woods, be prepared for the startling eruption of the American woodcock and its telltale zigzag flight through the trees. On the east bank of the lake is La Cygne Lake Wildlife Area. The entrance road is bordered by thick underbrush, ideal for a variety of winter sparrows and cottontail rabbits. Beaver gnawings are visible on the trees. Other habitats worth exploring are the wet meadows and woods below the dam along North Sugar Creek. Look for woodpeckers, warblers, owls, and other woodland animals.

Directions: La Cygne Lake lies 5 miles east of the town of La Cygne. To reach Linn County Park from U.S. 69, take the La Cygne Exit east 0.3 miles and follow the sign north 2 miles to the park entrance. The wildlife area is located 7.2 miles from U.S. 69. It is reached by traveling east across the dam and then north at the first intersection past the generating plant. The wildlife area lies 2 miles north and 1 mile west of this intersection. **Ownership:** Kansas City Power and Light, Inc.; also contact KDWP (913-352-8941); Linn County Park (913-757-6633) **4,600 acres**

P ✸✸ H₂0 ⚐ ⚑ ✸ ⚑ ⚑

Mike Blair

Always rare in Kansas, the trumpeter swan is becoming a winter visitor to reservoirs in the state. When this graceful and friendly bird arrives in Kansas it always makes headlines.

25 Marais des Cygnes Wildlife Area

"Marsh of the Swans" is what the early French trappers named the river from which this wetland emerged. Prehistoric-looking paddlefish make spring spawning runs in the river up to a low-water dam at Osawatomie. However, this site is best known for its abundant waterfowl—as many as 150,000 birds during fall and spring migrations. Common ducks include mallards, northern pintails, wigeons, blue-winged teal, green-winged teal, gadwalls, scaup, northern shovelers, and ring-necked ducks. Wood ducks and Canada geese nest in the area. Greater white-fronted geese and snow geese also stop. Including waterfowl, over 300 species of birds make this area popular with birders. Herons, egrets, eagles, shorebirds, hawks, and songbirds are plentiful. Visitors should pick up a map at the headquarters located on U.S. 69 about 1 mile north of Trading Post. The lake in Unit B, just west of the headquarters, is a great location to see large flocks of Canada geese and ducks as well as wintering bald eagles. From the headquarters, proceed south past Trading Post and cross the Marais des Cygnes River. Just south of the river, follow the gravel road west into the wildlife area as it passes next to the lake in Unit A. This is the largest pool in the area and is excellent for viewing great blue herons, white pelicans, and double-crested cormorants. In about 3 miles you will reach the small town of Boicourt. Prior to crossing the railroad tracks, turn north and follow the road as it parallels the river. During spring migration the steep woodlands are home to a variety of birds, including vireos, flycatchers, tanagers, orioles, and, sometimes, pileated woodpeckers. Over 30 species of warblers have been found here. A mile north of Boicourt lies Unit G of the wildlife area. The many stumps and trees protruding from the water's surface create ideal habitat for wood ducks, prothonotary warblers, migrating ospreys, and nesting tree swallows. In addition to the wetland, there are many areas with woodlands and open fields. Alert visitors may spot deer, gray foxes, turkeys, rabbits, and squirrels. Southern flying squirrels are also found here but are seldom seen. In late October and early November the fall colors of the trees on the hillsides are spectacular. For the reptile lover, there are many kinds of water turtles and snakes active in the warmer seasons.

The Marais des Cygnes National Wildlife Refuge is being developed near this site. Check with the U.S. Fish and Wildlife Service and the Kansas Department of Wildlife and Parks for the latest information about this exciting new refuge.

Directions: Marais des Cygnes Wildlife Area is located along U.S. 69, 5 miles north of Pleasanton. The headquarters building is about 1 mile north of the small town of Trading Post. **Ownership:** KDWP (913-352-8941) **7,235 acres** **P**

26 Dingus Natural Area

Originally acquired by the Nature Conservancy, Dingus Natural Area is now managed by the Kansas Ornithological Society. Because there are no trails, it takes some effort to explore the area. For many years the north hill has been known as Fern Hill because of the lush understory. Several species of ferns are found here, including the rare and unusual purple cliff brake. There is also an excellent stand of eastern deciduous woodlands. The uplands consist of mature oaks and hickories. Visitors may encounter deer, bobcats, squirrels, and birds characteristic of mature woodlands. Birding can be excellent during migrations, with warblers, vireos, tanagers, orioles, and flycatchers abundant. Nesting species include black-capped chickadees, tufted titmice, northern parula warblers, Kentucky warblers, summer tanagers, and several species of woodpeckers. Wild turkeys are also found in the area. In spring great blue herons are seen flying to a heronry located on private property to the south. During spring and summer an evening visit can be unforgettable. The woods echo with the sounds of whip-poor-wills, chuck-will's-widows, and barred owls. If there has been abundant rain and the roadside ditches hold standing water, the birds are joined by a chorus of amphibians. Vocal amphibians include Blanchard's cricket frogs, western chorus frogs, and gray treefrogs.

Directions: From Mound City take K-52 southwest about 3 miles to the top of the hill. Turn right at the Dingus Natural Area sign and follow the road north 1.5 miles and then west. There is a large sign on the southeast corner of the property. **Ownership:** Kansas Ornithological Society (913-795-2747) **166 acres** ▣

27 Yates Center Reservoir

Surrounded by upland native grasses, Yates Center Reservoir is an excellent place to get the "open tallgrass prairie feeling." Late spring and summer are the best times to view and photograph prairie wildflowers and birds. Commonly seen prairie birds include dickcissels, eastern meadowlarks, grasshopper sparrows, mourning doves, scissor-tailed flycatchers, and red-tailed hawks. On occasion upland sandpipers and greater prairie chickens are sighted. The lake attracts migrating waterfowl in spring and fall. If you visit in early spring, listen for western chorus frogs. In late spring and summer the deep bellow of a bullfrog is often heard. Basking on logs in the water are sliders and painted turtles.

Directions: To reach the lake, travel 4 miles southwest of Yates Center on U.S. 54, then 2 miles south and 0.25 miles east. There is no entry fee, but fees are required for fishing, boating, swimming, and camping. Write or call City Hall, 117 E. Rutledge, Yates Center KS 66783 (hours: M–F, 8–5). **Ownership:** City of Yates Center (316-625-2118) **500 acres**
▣

28 Woodson State Fishing Lake and Wildlife Area

Hiding in the Chautauqua Hills, just a few miles northeast of Toronto Reservoir, is enchanting little Woodson State Fishing Lake. It is surrounded by classic cross timbers, with dominant post and blackjack oak, big and little bluestem, sideoats grama, and Indiangrass. Upland bluestem prairie is prevalent in the adjacent Woodson Wildlife Area. On the east side of the lake the cool, wooded ravines are great for exploring. Ferns and mosses grow around the rocky outcroppings and clear pools formed by the dripping stream. In March and April watch for lesser scaup, goldeneyes, and buffleheads on the lake. Survey the shallows for great blue herons and the mudflats for least sandpipers and lesser and greater yellowlegs. The woodlands and thickets are inhabited by a variety of woodpeckers and songbirds. In early spring, you may hear the song of western chorus frogs coming from the lake's edge. From May into summer, listen for northern cricket frogs and bullfrogs calling from the lake and gray treefrogs from the prairie and woodland edge. Examine rocky sites for lizards, skinks, and snakes. Be alert for copperheads! Painted turtles and sliders may bask on logs in the water. Tracks of opossum, raccoon, and deer are frequently seen on the mudflats. Watch for these secretive mammals in the twilight hours. Listen at night for the barred owl, chuck-will's-widow, and the "yip yip yeowww" of the coyote. A variety of damselflies and dragonflies frequent the lake, and butterflies are found in the woods and grasslands. In the woodland edge and open prairie you may see raptors, mourning doves, and upland plovers. Blinds are available for spring viewing of greater prairie chickens. Call the Toronto/Fall River Unit Office at Toronto State Park (316-637-2213) for arrangements.

Directions: To reach the lake, travel 7 miles southwest of Yates Center on U.S. 54. Follow the gravel road south 3 miles, then east for 1.25 miles. **Ownership:** KDWP (316-637-2213) **2,850 acres** 🅿 ⚇ H₂0 ⋔ Ⓐ ⊛

Coyote sightings can occur anywhere in the state. Because of their secretive habits, they are more often heard than seen.

29 Toronto Reservoir

Toronto Reservoir lies in the scenic valley of the Verdigris River, just south of the village of Toronto. The cross timbers, riparian woodlands, grasslands, and stream and lake communities of the beautiful Chautauqua Hills region provide habitat for many wildlife species. Toronto Wildlife Area, located along the Verdigris River, Walnut Creek, and the north end of the lake, provides year-round viewing for white-tailed deer, red fox, raccoon, and turkey, particularly in the twilight hours. In summer, check the shallow waters for great blue herons. During spring and fall migrations many species of waterfowl can be seen on the lake. Plovers and sandpipers can be viewed on the northern and western mudflats. American white pelicans are common visitors to the open waters. Bald eagles perch and scavenge near the park office in winter. During summer, purple martins are seen around their houses at Toronto Point and Holiday Hill. Look to the sky and you will likely see circling turkey vultures. At Toronto Point is the 4-mile Toronto Park Trail, which passes around a small cove and through woodlands and sandy glades. Along the trail, at dawn or dusk any time of year, watch for deer, turkey, quail, coyotes, hawks, rabbits, and squirrels. From late spring to early fall, search for ornate box turtles, painted turtles, common garter snakes, and six-lined racerunners. Watch for copperheads!

Directions: To reach the Toronto State Park Office, go 12 miles west of Yates Center on U.S. 54 to K-105; travel south 9 miles on K-105, through Toronto, to the west side of the dam. Toronto Wildlife Area is about 2 miles west of K-105 on U.S. 54, then south along the west side of the Verdigris River. Park permits, trail information, and a wildlife area map are available at the Toronto State Park Office. **Ownership:** USACE (316-658-4445); KDWP (316-637-2213) **5,840 acres** P ♯♯ H$_2$0 ⵢ Ⓐ ♀ ♀♀ ⊜ ≈

The population of wood ducks continues to increase in Kansas. Although they normally nest in tree cavities, nest boxes placed in flooded timber or along streams and rivers are readily accepted as substitutes.

30 Fall River Reservoir

Good in any season! Situated in the rolling tallgrass prairies and wooded valleys of the Flint and Chautauqua hills, Fall River Reservoir is a picturesque site with diverse habitat. Fall River and its tributaries are lined with oak, hickory, walnut, elm, and hackberry trees. Grasses and wildflowers dominate the uplands. Ragweed, marestail, foxtail, annual and Maximilian sunflower are found around the edges of fields and along roadways. All provide food, cover, and reproduction places for more than 400 species of wildlife. Spring brings the booming of greater prairie chickens to the grasslands. Scissor-tailed flycatchers, Henslow's sparrows, eastern bluebirds, and northern orioles can be seen in spring and summer. Bald eagles are common in the Fredonia Bay area in winter. Canada geese are found year-round in Quarry Bay. The quarry is a great spot to look for reptiles. Wild turkey, deer, raccoons, bobcats, coyotes, fox squirrels, beaver, and northern bobwhite quail are year-round residents. In the woodlands are northern flickers and downy and pileated woodpeckers. During migrations waterfowl can be seen from the observation blind in the northeast part of the wildlife area. Expect to see bufflehead, scaup, mergansers, pintails, shovelers, and lots of mallards. The mudflats may produce American avocets, as well as sandpipers and plovers. Large flocks of white pelicans are sometimes seen on the open waters.

Directions: From K-96 at the north edge of Fall River, follow the signs north 3 miles to the dam. At the Corps of Engineers Information Center, on the west side of the dam, you can pick up maps, checklists, and other information. **Ownership:** USACE (316-658-4445); KDWP (316-637-2213) 10,270 acres $ **P** ✝✝ H_2O ✚ Ⓐ ⊜ ⇒

31 Bourbon State Fishing Lake and Wildlife Area

Aged to perfection! Located in the forest-prairie mosaic of the Osage Cuestas, Bourbon State Fishing Lake and Wildlife Area offers great wildlife viewing. Wolfpen Creek's woodland and shrubs along the hillsides provide cover and food for a variety of mammals and birds. The chatter of squirrels and the clear, crisp call of the northern bobwhite quail are commonly heard. Muskrats and mink are found in and near the water. Eastern cottontails and white-tailed deer can be seen throughout the area. The secretive American woodcock nests in the thickets; its presence is betrayed only by the springtime sound of a nasal "peent" at dawn or dusk. In May and September many species of wood warblers, as well as ducks, wading birds, and shorebirds, migrate through. Prairie wildflowers and butterflies are abundant from spring through fall. Painted turtles, sliders, bullfrogs, leopard frogs, and several species of water snakes are seen around the lake. Ground skinks are found in the rocky areas, with prairie kingsnakes and six-lined racerunners in the surrounding grasslands.

Directions: From Moran go 9 miles south on U.S. 59 to the Elsmore turnoff. Drive 5 miles straight east to the lake and wildlife area. **Ownership:** KDWP (316-362-3671) **277 acres** **P** ✝✝ H_2O ✚ Ⓐ ⇒

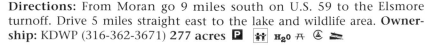

32 Crawford State Fishing Lake

Formed by a dam built on the West Fork of Dry Wood Creek in 1934 as a Civilian Conservation Corps project, Lake Crawford has long been home to a variety of wildlife. The oak-hickory and riparian woodlands, plus the surrounding grasslands and croplands, give the wildlife watcher opportunities to see dozens of animals, ranging from butterflies to birds. Commonly seen mammals include white-tailed deer, cottontail rabbits, squirrels, foxes, coyotes, bobcats, raccoons, and opossums. Ducks, geese, wading birds, and shorebirds can be seen on the lake during spring and fall. Scan the thickets for warblers during migrations. Nesting here are indigo buntings, northern cardinals, yellow-breasted chats, and Bell's vireos. Around the fields and prairies red-tailed hawks, northern harriers, dickcissels, grasshopper sparrows, and field sparrows can be viewed. Look for the broadhead skink, a threatened species in Kansas, in dead trees with woodpecker holes. Prairie lizards are found in the woodlands too. They will climb trees to escape as you approach. Be sure to visit Farlington Fish Hatchery just north of the dam.

Directions: Drive 9 miles north of Girard on K-7, then 1 mile east to the dam and information shelter. **Ownership:** KDWP (316-362-3671) **440 acres** ▣ ⚲ H₂0 ⊼ Ⓐ ⇋ ⊘

33 Mined Land Wildlife Area No. 1

Like gold! Strip-mining for coal in the early 1900s produced small lakes with low bordering ridges of wooded spoil banks that harbor a variety of wildlife. Cottonwood, elm, hackberry, ash, and oak provide habitat for woodland species. These include great horned owls, barred owls, screech-owls, bobwhite quail, wild turkeys, and numerous species of songbirds. Squirrels, deer, and foxes are also found in the woods. The mined lakes provide habitat for wood ducks, wading birds, beavers, muskrats, raccoons, and several species of water turtles. Of special interest is a small managed herd of bison on the northwest portion of the area.

Directions: Mined Land Wildlife Area No. 1 is located at the junction of U.S. 69 and U.S. 160 just north of Pittsburg. The area office is 3 miles west and 0.25 miles south of U.S. 69 bypass on 20th Street. For information and a map write Mined Land Wildlife Area Office, Route 2, Box 929, Pittsburg KS 66762. **Ownership:** KDWP (316-231-3173) **420 acres**

▣ ⇋ ⊘ Ⓐ

More than 420 bird species have been documented in Kansas. This diversity is due in part to the state's central location and variety of habitats.

34 Neosho Wildlife Area

In the broad valley of the Neosho River, just east of St. Paul, lie the 3,000-plus acres of Neosho Wildlife Area. Gar can often be seen feeding near the river's surface in summer. There are two species of this menacing, snouted fish here: longnosed and shortnosed. Spotted gar, the third variety, surfaces in the refuge pools. The managed marshes and the riparian woodlands provide habitat for diverse species of wildlife, particularly migrating waterfowl. Thousands of shorebirds, geese, and ducks are present during spring and fall migrations. Commonly seen ducks are green-winged and blue-winged teal, mallards, northern pintails, northern shovelers, buffleheads, and common goldeneyes. Between November and March, look for bald eagles perched in bare winter trees. Spring brings a variety of warblers, wrens, and vireos to the woodlands. Wood ducks nest in the area in summer. Pileated woodpeckers can be heard year-round in the mature woodlands. Search the marshes for muskrats and beavers. Wild turkeys and white-tailed deer are frequently seen. Southern flying squirrels inhabit the trees around Flatrock Creek but are seldom seen. A large variety of turtles may be seen here.

Directions: Neosho Wildlife Area lies on the south side of K-57, 1 mile east of St. Paul. **Ownership:** KDWP (316-362-3671) **3,246 acres**

35 Mined Land Wildlife Areas Nos. 20 to 23

Dig into this one! Years ago huge motorized shovels stripped the overburden of earth here so that underlying coal could be removed. Over time the land has become a rough and rolling tract of shrublands, woodlands, and grasslands weaving around long deep lakes and numerous small pits. Cottonwood, elm, hackberry, and oaks compose the woodlands. Native bluestems, switchgrass, and Indiangrass have been planted as part of the wildlife management plan. An area office is located on unit 21 as is a 30-acre Canada goose restoration pen. The geese can be viewed year-round. Many species of dabbling and diving ducks, as well as osprey, can be seen during spring and fall migrations. In winter bald eagles are occasionally sighted around the lakes. Northern harriers are commonly seen over the grasslands. Several species of water turtles, beaver, muskrats, and raccoons are abundant around the pits throughout the year. The woodlands hold squirrels, owls, wild turkeys, and many songbirds. Watch in the evening and early morning for foxes, coyotes, bobcats, bobwhite quail, cottontail rabbits, and white-tailed deer. Deer Trace Canoe Trail has been developed through these areas.

Directions: From the junction of K-96 and K-7 at Columbus, drive 7 miles west on K-96. Travel 4 miles north, then 0.5 miles west to get to units 20–23. For information on Mined Land Wildlife Areas write Mined Land Wildlife Area Office, Route 2, Box 188, Columbus KS 66725. **Ownership:** KDWP (316-827-6135) **2,000 acres**

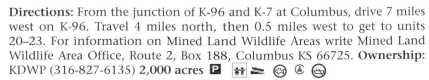

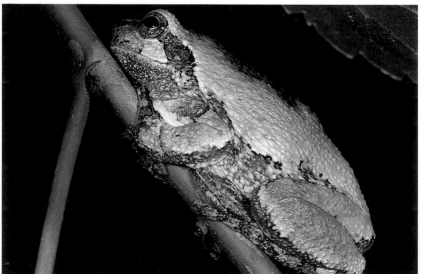

36 Schermerhorn Park

Like Dorothy, you might think you're not in Kansas any more as you explore Schermerhorn Park, just south of Galena, in the 50-square-mile "Ozarks of Kansas." The hillsides, dominated by white and Shumard's oaks and bitternut and shagbark hickories, are typically Ozarkian. Many of the state's threatened and endangered species live in this region. Rare fish found here include the Ozark minnow, black redhorse, and greenside darter. The Mississippian limestone of the area contains numerous caves with small outflowing streams, providing homes for the cave salamander. At the twilight zone of Schermerhorn Cave the brilliant orange cave salamander moves through rock wall crevices in search of insects. Streams and small marshes are the habitats of the spring peeper, pickerel frog, and green frog. Gray myotis, eastern pipistrelle, big brown, and red bats live in the area. These species are protected by law and should be left alone. Watchable wildlife includes ornate box turtles, five-lined skinks, slider and painted turtles, white-tailed deer, eastern chipmunks, and gray and fox squirrels. In late summer evenings, listen for chuck-will's-widows, whip-poor-wills, great horned owls, barred owls, and eastern screech-owls and the high-pitched chirp of flying squirrels. With a flashlight you might be able to see this nocturnal rodent gracefully glide from tree branch to nearby tree base, climb up, and glide again. Woodland birds found in this area include red-shouldered hawks, pileated woodpeckers, Carolina chickadees, scarlet tanagers, and yellow-throated warblers.

Directions: Go 1 mile south of Galena on K-26. The park is on the east side of the road just before you reach Shoal Creek bridge. Be careful, this stretch of road is very steep! **Ownership:** City of Galena (316-783-5265) 24 acres 🅿 ♀♂ H₂0 ⋔ 🚶

Gray tree frogs have large pads on the tips of their toes, which enable them to cling to the vertical surfaces of leaves and small branches. They vary in color from gray to bright green.

Bob Gress

37 Big Hill Reservoir

The beautiful Big Hill Creek valley is the setting for this reservoir. Located in an oak-bluestem forest, commonly called the cross timbers, the area provides a wide variety of native vegetation and wildlife. Nixon and Pfeil trails take you through woodlands of post, blackjack, red, and chinquapin oaks. Their acorns provide nutrition for wild turkey, gray squirrels, and fox squirrels. Look for deer trails and watch for cardinals, chickadees, blue jays, and woodpeckers. Armadillos, woodchucks, red and gray foxes, and bobcats can also be found here. In spring, listen in the evening and early morning for great horned owls, whip-poor-wills, and chuck-will's-widow. In early summer watch for eastern bluebirds, American redstarts, Carolina wrens, and Kentucky warblers. Big Hill Wildlife Area, in the uplands, contains grasslands and hedgerows. Bluestem prairie grasses and wildflowers such as woolly verbena, green and butterfly milkweed, western yarrow, partridge pea, spreading aster, and dotted gayfeather provide habitat for mice, cottontails, and coyotes. Hedgerows of osage orange, dogwood, and persimmon furnish nesting sites for Bell's vireo, orchard orioles, northern bobwhite quail, and scissor-tailed flycatchers. Reptile lovers may find ornate box turtles, six-lined racerunners, five-lined skinks, great plains rat, and ringneck snakes. In wooded areas be alert for copperheads. During migrations check the lake for snow and Canada geese, canvasbacks, redheads, pintails, and blue-winged teal. Branum Horse Trail for equestrians loops around the northern part of the lake.

Directions: To get to Big Hill Reservoir dam, take U.S. 169 to Main Street in Cherryvale. Turn east and go to the end of Main. Go south 1 block, then 4 miles east. Maps and other information are available at the Corps of Engineers Information Center on the west side of the dam. The horse trail starts just south of U.S. 160 about 1.5 miles west of Dennis. **Ownership:** USACE (316-336-2741); KDWP (316-331-6820) **2,560 acres**

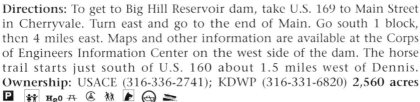

38 Montgomery State Fishing Lake

South of Independence, just a mile before Coal Creek empties into the Verdigris River, is Montgomery State Fishing Lake. The lake's marshlands, riparian woodlands, and surrounding grasslands provide habitat for many species of wildlife. Diving ducks (such as ring-necked, common goldeneye, and bufflehead) can be seen on the lake in winter and early spring. Look in the marshy areas for mallards, pintails, muskrats, and beaver. The woodlands hold woodpeckers, northern cardinals, and blue jays, and bluebirds are common in open areas. Warblers pass through in spring and fall. Vireos and indigo buntings nest in summer. In evening and early morning watch for wild turkey, white-tailed deer, and fox squirrels. Meadowlarks, dickcissels, grasshopper sparrows, mourning doves, and northern harriers can be observed on the grasslands.

Directions: From the junction of U.S. 75 and U.S. 160 in Independence, travel 4 miles south on Tenth Street (County Road 3900). Turn east; drive 1 mile to the lake. **Ownership:** KDWP (316-331-6295) **408 acres**

39 Elk City Reservoir

The undulating grasslands and timbered valleys of the Osage Cuestas make Elk City Reservoir one of the most exquisite spots in Kansas. Miles of National Recreation Trails provide spectacular vistas of the lake and wind through some of the most appealing rock formations in the state. November through March are great months to see thousands of snow geese and their greater white-fronted and Canada cousins grazing the wheat fields near the wildlife refuge. Winter woodland birds include kinglets, brown creepers, tufted titmice, white-breasted nuthatches, and Carolina chickadees. Bald eagles, common and popular winter residents, can be best viewed in the standing timber of the backwaters of the upper reaches of the lake, particularly near Card Creek campground. Look for wood ducks there also. During spring and summer watch for woodpeckers, blue jays, and flycatchers. Neotropical birds, such as indigo and painted buntings, summer tanagers, northern parula, and prothonotary warblers, nest in this area. Ducks and large flocks of American white pelicans migrate through here. The woods are inhabited by pileated woodpeckers and red-tailed hawks year-round. Gray treefrogs, collared lizards, five-lined skinks, and ringneck snakes are active in spring and summer. Deer, squirrels, rabbits, wild turkeys, gray foxes, beavers, and raccoons are sometimes seen in the early morning and evening hours.

Directions: Travel 1 mile west of Independence on U.S. 160. Follow the signs about 3 miles to the park office. The Corps of Engineers Information Center is a little over 3 miles northwest of the park office, just west of the dam. Maps, trail guides, and permits are available at both locations. **Ownership:** USACE (316-331-0315); KDWP (316-331-6295) **13,000 acres**

$ P 👫 H₂O ⛽ Ⓒ 🥾 👫 🚴 🌳 🚤

The beautiful indigo bunting breeds throughout the state. Arriving from Mexico and the West Indies in May, these riparian woodland inhabitants usually produce two broods of young before returning to their wintering grounds in late September.

Gene Brehm

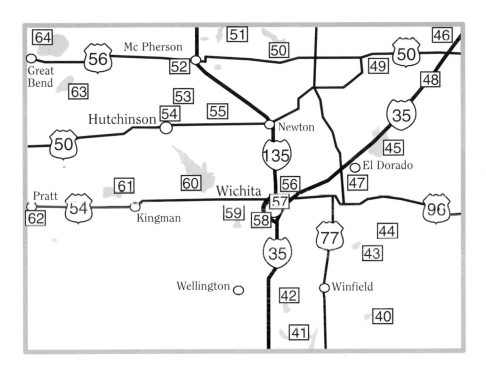

40 Cowley State Fishing Lake
41 Chaplin Nature Center
42 Slate Creek Wildlife Area
43 Winfield City Lake
44 Butler State Fishing Lake
45 El Dorado Reservoir
46 Prairie Chicken Viewing Blinds
47 Flint Hills Wildlife Drive
48 Cattle Pens
49 Chase State Fishing Lake
50 Marion Reservoir
51 Maxwell Wildlife Area and McPherson State Fishing Lake
52 McPherson Valley Wetlands

53 Sand Hills State Park
54 Dillon Nature Center
55 Harvey County West Park
56 Chisholm Creek Park
57 Wichita Rivers
58 Pawnee Prairie Park
59 Lake Afton
60 Cheney Reservoir
61 Byron Walker Wildlife Area
62 Pratt Fish Hatchery
63 Quivira National Wildlife Refuge
64 Cheyenne Bottoms Wildlife Area

40 Cowley State Fishing Lake

Cowley State Fishing Lake attracts wildlife from the surrounding tallgrass prairie. Upland sandpipers, common nighthawks, and eastern meadowlarks are common throughout the summer. The trees surrounding the lake attract migrating songbirds as well as a few nesters, including northern orioles, kingbirds, robins, and mourning doves. Collared lizards, slender glass lizards, and tarantulas are frequently found around the exposed limestone boulders, and occasionally you may be surprised by a venomous copperhead. For naturalists, the area is most attractive for its spectacular wildflower blooms. In spring look for rose verbena, prairie spiderwort, ground-plum, and Oklahoma phlox. Kaw Wildlife Area, located just a few miles from the lake, often produces some unexpected finds. For an interesting drive to several good wildlife spots, travel 6.4 miles west of Cowley State Fishing Lake on U.S. 166 to Cowley County 1. Turn south and head toward Silverdale. Along the road look for loggerhead shrikes, scissor-tailed flycatchers, and dickcissels. This area also harbors one of the largest populations of bobcats in the state, although they are rarely seen. Just south of Silverdale, alfalfa fields flank both sides of the road. In late April and early May, bobolinks are frequently found here. Two bridges span Grouse Creek, and both sites are marked as parts of Kaw Wildlife Area. In spring these riparian woodlands are full of warblers, vireos, and flycatchers. A rock road heads west 1.3 miles south of Silverdale; follow this road through blackjack and post oak country for 3.3 miles. Watch for white-tailed deer and wild turkeys. During spring, the night woods are alive with the calls of chuck-will's-widows. Across the road from Horizon Methodist Center is a second-growth woodland that usually has singing painted buntings, indigo buntings, and blue grosbeaks in late April and May. This is private property, but the birds can usually be seen and heard from the road. Cowley County 6 is at the stop sign another mile north of Camp Horizon. Two miles west is another entrance to Kaw Wildlife Area. Here the Arkansas River can be scanned for wintering bald eagles or springtime ducks and shorebirds.

Directions: Cowley State Fishing Lake lies 13 miles east of Arkansas City on U.S. 166. **Ownership:** KDWP (316-321-7180) **197 acres**

P 👫 H₂0 ⚘ Ⓐ 🛶

White-tailed deer are the most common deer in Kansas. The spots on this young fawn will remain until fall.

41 Chaplin Nature Center

Chaplin Nature Center is located along the sandy beaches of the Arkansas River. Five miles of walking trails provide easy access to bottomland timber, prairies, a spring-fed creek, and the Arkansas River. The varied habitat has attracted 225 species of birds, including tree sparrows, Harris' sparrows, rufous-sided towhees, cedar waxwings, and Carolina wrens. The woodlands harbor a good diversity of tree species, including black walnut, pecan, cottonwood, sycamore, red elm, and a showy springtime display of redbuds. Pileated woodpeckers inhabit the bottomlands, along with wood thrushes, wild turkeys, bobcats, and white-tailed deer. The rough green snake, a favorite of reptile lovers, is sometimes seen. A popular wintertime activity is watching bald eagles from the riverbanks. The visitor center features wildlife displays, a nature library, a gift shop, and a bird-observation area located on a second-floor open deck bordered by tree canopy and serviced with bird feeders. It provides an ideal spot for bird photography or birdwatching from the comfort of the library. In winter you may see white-breasted nuthatches, downy woodpeckers, red-bellied woodpeckers, American goldfinches, dark-eyed juncos, and northern cardinals. In summer ruby-throated hummingbirds frequent the feeders and eastern bluebirds use the nest boxes provided. For the wildlife watcher, a visit to Chaplin Nature Center guarantees success.

Directions: From the intersection of U.S. 77 and U.S. 166 in Arkansas City, travel 3 miles west on U.S. 166, then north 2 miles. Signs are provided for assistance. **Ownership:** Wichita Audubon Society (316-442-4133)

200 acres 🅿 🚻 H₂0 🌲 🏕 🚶 🚶‍♂️

42 Slate Creek Wildlife Area

Slate Creek is only for the strong-willed! This wetland cannot be entered by automobile road, and visitors should be prepared for some hiking. The property provides an interesting mix of habitats—woodland, cropland, and native prairie, as well as the wetland. The flat terrain makes the shallow pools and mudflats difficult to see from the parking areas. During dry periods, much of the area may be completely dry. The area is the permanent home of white-tailed deer, coyotes, raccoons, and muskrats. The best time to visit is probably in spring and fall when the waterfowl and shorebirds are migrating. Large numbers of white-rumped and Baird's sandpipers visit in spring. Wilson's phalaropes, greater and lesser yellowlegs, long-billed dowitchers, and killdeers are also found. Most of the puddle ducks found in Kansas feed here, and great blue herons commonly feed in the shallows. LeConte's sparrows occur regularly.

Directions: From U.S. 160 in Oxford, go 7.2 miles south on Summer Street. Turn west at the Slate Valley Baptist Church, and travel another 1.6 miles to a parking area on the north side of the road. Some of the wetland area lies northwest of this parking lot. Two other parking areas can be reached by driving the perimeter of the property. **Ownership:** KDWP (316-321-7180) **667 acres** 🅿

43 Winfield City Lake

This one's a winner! Most of the lake is surrounded by tallgrass prairie, but the north shore has wooded draws, hedgerows, and brushy areas. Nesting birds include scissor-tailed flycatchers, common poor-wills, upland sandpipers, common grackles, and northern orioles. During the winter eastern bluebirds are attracted to the open, grassy park areas surrounding the lake. Wintering Harris' sparrows are quite abundant in brushy areas. A nice stand of deciduous woodland graces the far eastern end where Timber Creek flows into the lake. Watch for white-tailed deer, turkeys, and other woodland birds, including common flickers, tufted titmice, Carolina chickadees, and northern cardinals. Along the hedgerows look for the large stick nests of eastern wood rats, sometimes called "pack rats." The cattail marshes and mudflats on the east end attract an assortment of blackbirds, herons, and shorebirds during migrations. During the winter, Winfield City Lake is thought to be a good spot for viewing uncommon waterfowl, including loons and scoters. Typical winter waterfowl include common mergansers, buffleheads, mallards, and common goldeneyes. The best places to scan the lake are the high bluffs along the south shore. Both North and South Shore Recreation Areas are easily accessible by road.

Directions: From the intersection of U.S. 160 and U.S. 77 in Winfield, travel north 8.7 miles on U.S. 77. Follow the sign east 6.4 miles on Cowley County 8. **Ownership:** City of Winfield (316-221-4249) **2,000 acres** 🅿 🚻 ⛱ ♿ 🛥

Although it's rare to see beaver, their signs are certainly visible. Beaver dams create important habitat for fish, muskrats, and waterfowl.

44 Butler State Fishing Lake

This peaceful retreat lies in the heart of the Flint Hills tallgrass prairie. During spring and fall the lake offers one of the area's few stopovers for migrating ducks—among them American wigeons, blue-winged teal, mallards, buffleheads, lesser scaup, and northern shovelers. Anglers are entertained by painted turtles, bullfrogs, chorus frogs, and dragonflies cruising the shoreline for small insects. At both ends of the lake, small wooded areas adjoin the North Branch of Rock Creek. Beaver cuttings are evident, as are the bushy leaf nests of fox squirrels. Bobwhites, cardinals, chickadees, woodpeckers, and other woodland birds are concentrated along this riparian corridor. Purple prairie clover, catclaw sensitive brier, blue false indigo, and yellow prairie coneflower are just a few of the many wildflowers that bloom in the rolling hills around the lake. Greater prairie chicken booming grounds (leks) on the surrounding prairie can be located on still spring mornings by driving slowly along country roads at sunrise and stopping frequently to listen for the displaying males. Other prairie birds include upland sandpipers, common nighthawks, loggerhead shrikes, and eastern meadowlarks. Be alert for deer and coyotes. Bobcats are also here but are seldom seen.

Directions: Butler State Fishing Lake is located 2 miles north and 2 miles west of Latham. **Ownership:** KDWP (316-321-7180) **546 acres**

45 El Dorado Reservoir

To wildlife watchers, habitat diversity is the key to a successful outing. El Dorado Reservoir, in addition to extensive open water and flooded timber, also has adjacent croplands, woodlands, and rocky outcroppings. The dominant habitat, however, is the surrounding tallgrass prairie. In spring, the area is rich with wildflowers. Stop by the administration building southeast of the dam to pick up a map. You may want to circle the lake. Each area offers its own wildlife specialty. The prairie around Shady Creek is a good spot for meadowlarks, greater prairie chickens, and common nighthawks. Deer are also seen here and in the wooded areas east of K-177 where Shady Creek and Bemis Creek flow into the lake. Bluestem Point may provide one of the best opportunities for wildlife viewing. In winter "tame" Canada geese are often encountered along the roads. Bald eagles commonly perch in flooded timber north of the campgrounds. This unique habitat supports prothonotary warblers and tree swallows in spring. Below the dam, the Walnut River area provides woodlands that support cardinals, chickadees, and woodpeckers. Hawks and vultures ride the thermals near the dam, and mink are sometimes seen among the rocks at the water's edge. The park road through the Boulder Bluff Area ends at an old rock quarry. There, during the warmer months, collared lizards often sun themselves on the large rocks. In winter stop along the road in areas that provide good views and check the dead trees in the water for perched bald eagles. Winter also provides large numbers of visible waterfowl.

Directions: From U.S. 77, at the north end of the city of El Dorado, follow the signs 2 miles east to the dam. K-177, 5 miles east of El Dorado, also provides several access points. **Ownership:** USACE (316-321-9974); KDWP (316-321-7180) **16,000 acres** 🅿 ♀♂ H₂0 ⛱ Ⓒ 🚶 🛥

Kansas harbors more prairie chickens–around 15,000– than any other state in the nation. Public observation blinds make prairie chicken booming grounds available to anyone.

Kansas contains more prairie chickens than any other state. The plum-colored neck sacs of the lesser prairie chicken are visible on the males only during the spring breeding season when they gather on leks to perform their spectacular dancing displays.

46 Prairie Chicken Viewing Blinds

The annual mating ritual of the prairie chicken is one of nature's most impressive displays! Around mid-March, prairie chickens begin gathering on booming grounds, also known as leks. The males engage in dancing and other courtship behaviors designed to establish dominance and to attract females. Although lek activity may continue through early May, it usually peaks during the first two weeks of April. Watch for coyotes and other predators that hunt prairie chickens. The Kansas Department of Wildlife and Parks operates several viewing blinds during the spring. Most of these are located in the tallgrass prairie region. Additional blinds are being developed. The blinds typically hold four to six people and must be entered at least one-half hour before sunrise. Reservations are required.

Directions: Blinds may occupy different leks in different years, so to check blind availability and location contact KDWP: Pratt office, 316-672-5911; Valley Center office, 316-755-2711; Emporia office, 316-342-0658.
P

47 Flint Hills Wildlife Drive

Get a real taste for the tallgrass prairie that once stretched across much of the Midwest and eastern Great Plains. Much of the remaining prairie is in the Flint Hills, an area approximately 40 miles wide stretching through Kansas from northern Oklahoma to Nebraska. This grassland sea is characterized by four dominant species: big bluestem, little bluestem, Indiangrass, and switchgrass. Our 58-mile drive takes travelers into the heart of the area. The vistas are some of the most scenic in the country. The rock roads are sometimes rough. Please remember that the property is private, and your exploration should be limited to the roadways. Coyotes may be encountered throughout the year. Raptors include red-tailed hawks, northern harriers, and American kestrels. During winter they may be joined by prairie falcons and rough-legged hawks. During spring and summer watch for upland sandpipers, common nighthawks, eastern meadowlarks, loggerhead shrikes, and grasshopper sparrows. These hills also harbor the largest population of greater prairie chickens in the world. The best times to visit are during spring and fall. Spring provides numerous wildflowers in addition to the wildlife. In fall, the bluestem grasses show their subtle hues of blue and red.

Directions: Begin in the town of Cassoday—"prairie chicken capital of the world." Travel south; where K-177 curves to the southwest, continue straight over the railroad tracks, past the old high school and water tower. Take the first road east; at 1 mile, jog to the south, and in another 0.5 miles turn back to the east. Continue into the Flint Hills for another 7 miles to two large ponds. Just below the dams, take the left turn and continue east. In another 7.6 miles you will arrive at the small town of Lapland (three or four houses). At the stop sign, turn left (north) and travel 4.5 miles to the next stop sign. Continue north across the intersection and past the many oil wells 4.5 miles to an intersection at the top of a hill. Turn left (west) and travel another 5.5 miles to the next intersection. This road is one of the most scenic in the area! Turn right at this intersection and travel north another 2.6 miles. Remember this intersection; if you take the following side trip into another very scenic region of the Flint Hills you will eventually return to this spot. Turn right (east). At the top of the hill, just past the AT&T microwave tower, turn left. At 6.1 miles from the side trip intersection Camp Creek joins the Verdigris River—an ideal spot to take a break. Both waterways are crystal clear and shallow. Backtrack 6.1 miles to the original intersection; continue west for 0.5 miles and then turn north onto Sharpes Creek Road. The town of Bazaar, 11 miles north, marks the end of the drive. Follow the paved road west through Bazaar to K-177. **Ownership:** Private

> *Pronghorns are now commonly seen near the cattle pens along I-35 in the heart of the Flint Hills.*

The Flint Hills region is the largest remaining tract of tallgrass prairie anywhere in the world.

48 Cattle Pens

This site is included not for its cow-watching attributes but because it is the easternmost location in Kansas to view pronghorns—often called antelope. The pronghorn is the fastest mammal in Kansas, capable of reaching speeds of nearly 70 mph. The current Kansas population of approximately 1,500 is only a fraction of the numbers that once roamed the prairies of Kansas with vast herds of bison. There are more than 100 pronghorns in this herd and they are often seen within 2 miles on either side of the cattle pens, usually on the north side of the interstate. The animals' presence is the result of re-establishment efforts sponsored by the Wichita and Kansas City chapters of Safari Club International and the Kansas Department of Wildlife and Parks. Many of these pronghorns are radio-collared and wear eartags. While traveling through this area be alert for coyotes and watch for the flapping-gliding flight of prairie chickens. Other tallgrass prairie birds, frequently seen perched on fence posts, include upland sandpipers, eastern meadowlarks, common nighthawks, American kestrels, and the always visible red-tailed hawks. Roadcuts along the interstate expose the Permian-age limestones containing many bands of chert or flint. During May and June these roadcuts are good locations to find the large yellow blossoms of the Missouri evening primrose. These showy flowers open at night and are usually closed by late morning. The cattle pens, located in the heart of the Flint Hills on I-35 near Bazaar, provide a place for local ranchers to corral cattle prior to shipping.

Directions: The cattle pens are located on I-35, 18.6 miles northeast of the Cassoday turnpike entrance and 16.4 miles southwest of the Emporia entrance. **Ownership:** Private

49 Chase State Fishing Lake

This beautiful lake is an ideal spot from which to hike the tallgrass prairie and explore the limestone-capped hilltops. Springtime sprinkles the countryside with colorful wildflowers. In the spring and summer, the large flat rocks on the hillsides are ideal hiding spots for reptiles. Look for collared lizards, Great Plains skinks, ringneck snakes, prairie kingsnakes, and racers. If you search under the rocks be sure to replace them in the same position that you found them. The many burrows, holes, and cavities under the rocks take years to develop and are a small but important habitat to a wide variety of reptiles, small mammals, and invertebrates. Spring birds bring a variety of sounds to the lake area. Listen for the wolf-whistle call of the upland sandpiper, the insect-like buzz of the grasshopper sparrow, and the melodious call of the eastern meadowlark. Other frequently seen birds include common nighthawks, northern harriers, and American kestrels. The trees around the lake also attract woodpeckers, orioles, robins, and flycatchers. During spring and fall migrations, the lake attracts a variety of ducks, and a few Canada geese usually overwinter here. For campers, nighttime often brings the calls of the common poorwills, which nest on the open ground amid the rocky outcroppings. You are likely to hear coyotes before morning and may see bobcats below the dam.

Directions: From K-177 in Cottonwood Falls travel west on Main Street 2.6 miles to the lake entrance. **Ownership:** KDWP (316-767-5900) **383 acres**

50 Marion Reservoir

One of the main attractions of Marion Reservoir is the large variety of water birds. During spring and fall migrations, large numbers of ducks, geese, white pelicans, and gulls can be seen on the open water. In summer, great blue herons and belted kingfishers are found. Cottonwood Point Recreation Area offers a good view of the reservoir. During summer, robins, eastern and western kingbirds, and northern orioles nest in the trees throughout the campground. Though visitors are not allowed to enter the Marion Goose Refuge (on the west side of the reservoir), flocks of Canada geese that winter there can be seen from the road. In the riparian woodlands of Marion Wildlife Area you can see white-tailed deer early in the morning. During spring and summer search the cattails for yellow-headed blackbirds, which are often seen flashing their white marked wings and heard calling in their rasping voices.

Directions: Marion Reservoir is located 4 miles west of Marion on U.S. 56. Follow the signs north on the paved road to the dam. Cottonwood Point Recreation Area is reached by traveling 1 mile north and 1 mile west of the north end of the dam. Marion Goose Refuge lies 2 miles west, then 1 mile north of the southwest end of the dam. To reach Marion Wildlife Area travel 4 miles west and 6 miles north of the southwest end of the dam. **Ownership:** USACE (316-382-2101); KDWP (316-732-3551) **12,500 acres**

51 Maxwell Wildlife Area and McPherson State Fishing Lake

The 4 square miles of Maxwell Wildlife Area and adjacent McPherson State Fishing Lake provide one of the best viewing opportunities in the state for large mammals. Today at Maxwell approximately 200 bison and 50 elk give visitors a rare look into the past. The observation tower is a good place to scan the rolling hills for wildlife. Visitors on the preserve are not allowed to leave the roadway by vehicle or by foot. If bison are on the road, view them from the safety of your vehicle. One of the most impressive times to experience the elk is during the rutting, or breeding, season. From mid-September until mid-October the dominant bulls are gathering cows into harems. Their bugling can be best heard on calm mornings and evenings. The area around McPherson State Fishing Lake is ideal for prairie wildflowers. In May and June there are impressive displays of yucca, spiderwort, catclaw sensitive brier, purple prairie clover, and coneflowers. Numerous butterfly milkweeds attract insects and butterflies, including the large, rare, regal fritillary butterfly. An eastern bluebird trail consists of numerous nesting boxes attached to a tall fence. While traveling the roads or exploring the prairie be alert for the plentiful ornate box turtles. Lizards such as six-lined racerunners and legless, slender glass lizards are also found here. Common snakes include black rat snakes, bullsnakes, and prairie kingsnakes. At the southwest corner of the lake is the Gypsum Creek Nature Trail. Watch for white-tailed deer, cottontail rabbits, fox squirrels, and woodland birds. Beaver sign is impressively abundant on this trail. If you walk slowly and quietly at night and use a strong flashlight you may gain some insight into the secret life of the largest Kansas rodent.

Directions: The entrance to Maxwell Wildlife Area and McPherson State Fishing Lake lies 6 miles north of Canton and 5 miles south of Roxbury on McPherson County 304. **Ownership:** KDWP (316-767-5900) **2,500 acres** P ♿ ⅌ Ⓐ 🚶 ⬌

Once the "bugle call" of thousands of elk (or wapiti, Shawnee for "pale rump") heralded the onset of autumn on the ancient prairie. Today elk can be seen only in a few small managed herds.

52 McPherson Valley Wetlands

Here are some wetlands on the rebound! Prior to 1880, more than 125 square miles of wetlands existed in the McPherson Valley. These marshes, formed at the end of the Ice Age, were second in importance only to Cheyenne Bottoms in providing sustenance to waterfowl and water birds migrating through Kansas. At the turn of the century the marshes were drained and the land was turned over to agriculture. Lake Inman (the largest natural lake in Kansas), Clear Pond, and a few small marshes are all that is left of the wetlands. In 1989 the Kansas Department of Wildlife and Parks, Ducks Unlimited, and the U.S. Fish and Wildlife Service jointly began to acquire land (on a willing-seller basis) and restore it to wetlands. Clear Pond and Lake Inman are, at this time, the best sites for viewing migrating waterfowl and water birds. Watch for ducks: northern pintails, American wigeons, northern shovelers, mallards, green-winged teal, ring-necked ducks, lesser scaup, blue-winged teal, redheads, buffleheads, and common goldeneyes. Geese are common. Watch also for sandpipers, plovers, herons, cormorants, and pelicans.

Directions: To reach Lake Inman, travel 3 miles east from K-61 at Inman, then 0.75 miles north. To get to Clear Pond, from U.S. 58 at McPherson travel 2.5 miles north on Lindsborg Road, then 4.5 miles west. A viewing blind is available at Clear Pond. **Ownership:** KDWP (316-767-5900) **1,310 acres** (with pending expansions) **P**

53 Sand Hills State Park

More sand than many deserts! Located on the north edge of the Hutchinson Dune Tract, Sand Hills State Park is a rolling sand prairie displaying hues of red, yellow, gray, lavender, and green. Dunes formed by wind-deposited sands from the Arkansas River at the end of the Ice Age have been stabilized by the roots of the sand prairie grasses. These include big sandreed, which quickly colonizes loose sands and allows the establishment of sand bluestem, sand dropseed, little bluestem, and switchgrass. Between the grasses grow woody shrubs and a variety of wildflowers, such as purple poppy mallow and goatsbeard. To get a feel for the park, take the hiking trail through the dunes. From late spring to early fall watch for several kinds of lizards. You probably will see badger holes and the little mounds of the plains pocket gopher. Be alert for quail and pheasant. After touring the south site, drive to the north parking lot on 69th Street. Walk the sloughs and marshes filled with sedges, rushes, and prairie cordgrass. In April and May listen for the music of the western chorus frogs. Look for blue cardinal flowers, swamp milkweeds, and lady's tresses orchids. The woodland trail is a good place to find bluebirds and blue grosbeaks. Deer, coyotes, owls, and hawks are common residents of the park. Nesting birds include orchard orioles, yellow-billed cuckoos, Bell's vireos, and mourning doves.

Directions: To reach the south parking lot of the park, take K-61 northeast of Hutchinson to 56th Street. Go east 0.3 miles. The north parking lot is 1 mile north of 56th on 69th Street. **Ownership:** KDWP (316-663-5272) **1,123 acres** **P** 🚻 ⛅ 🚶 🚶

Mike Blair

The aptly named butterfly milkweed attracts butterflies and other insects. Look for this beautiful plant between May and August at tall and mixed grass prairie sites in the eastern two-thirds of the state.

54 Dillon Nature Center

This National Urban Wildlife Sanctuary, operated by the Hutchinson Recreation Commission, is a demonstration area for attracting wildlife to urban settings. The Education and Discovery Center contains exhibits, a nature library, class and meeting rooms, and a gift shop. Butterfly and hummingbird gardens, birdhouses and feeders, and special displays give visitors many ideas on attracting wildlife to their yards. The more than 30-acre tract is a wild arboretum with hundreds of species of trees, shrubs, vines, grasses, and wildflowers. Trails wind through woods and prairies and by ponds and marshes. Bullfrogs, leopard frogs, sliders, and painted turtles can be viewed around the water. Also watch for Canada geese, pied-billed grebes, green herons, wood ducks, and spotted sandpipers. Interesting snakes of the area include the common garter, coachwhip, prairie kingsnake, and western hognose. Coyotes, foxes, cottontail rabbits, and white-tailed deer are often sighted. Mourning doves, yellow-billed cuckoos, great horned owls, common nighthawks, and several species of swallows, woodpeckers, and warblers can be seen at various seasons. Ospreys fish the ponds in October, and house finches, American goldfinches, and black-capped chickadees are at the feeding stations in winter.

Directions: In Hutchinson take K-61 to 30th Avenue. Dillon Nature Center is located less than a block east on 30th Avenue. **Ownership:** City of Hutchinson (316-663-7411) **30 acres** P 🚻 H₂0 🌲 🏛 🚶 🚶

55 Harvey County West Park

Harvey County West Park is "an old-fashioned country park" on the Little Arkansas River, at the northern edge of the Arkansas River Lowlands. The habitats are riparian woodlands, a small lake and pond, and sand prairie. Start your visit with a hike on the excellent 1-mile, self-guided Lakeside Nature Trail. The sand prairie is an area of sand dunes stabilized by the roots of bluestem grasses, sand lovegrass, and sandhill plum. The surface-bulging tunnels of eastern moles and mounds of dirt left by plains pocket gophers are signs of mammals seldom seen. However, pleasant, moonless nights will bring kangaroo rats from the fan-shaped entrance of their burrows. In summer, gaze overhead for turkey vultures, red-tailed hawks, and Mississippi kites. Hovering and swooping over the grasses are American kestrels, scissor-tailed flycatchers, and northern harriers. Colorful dragonflies and damselflies, whirligig and diving beetles, and water striders occupy the aquatic areas. Many kinds of amphibians and reptiles supply amusement: tiger salamanders, diamondback water snakes, spiny softshell turtles, and common snapping turtles. Other reptiles commonly seen in the dunes are western hognose snakes, plains garter snakes, six-lined racerunners, slender glass lizards, and ornate box turtles. View red-winged blackbirds, great blue herons, mallard ducks, beavers, and raccoons. In the woodlands of cottonwood, elm, hackberry, buckbrush, and rough-leaved dogwood are vireos, warblers, and thrushes. In winter Harris' sparrows, winter wrens, and red-breasted nuthatches are seen. Wild turkeys, white-tailed deer, opossums, and cottontail rabbits are always active.

Directions: Go 4 miles east of Burrton on U.S. 50 to Harvey County Road 793. Turn north, go 3 miles to Harvey County Road 566. The park entrance is about 0.8 miles east on the north side of the road. **Ownership:** Harvey County (316-835-3189) **310 acres** P H_2O

The red fox inhabits many urban parks in Kansas. These enchanting night hunters feed on rabbits, mice, berries, and insects.

56 Chisholm Creek Park

Made for wildlife—and humans! Chisholm Creek Park, in northeast Wichita, contains over 2 miles of paved, wheelchair-accessible nature trails. The trails wind through riparian woodlands, native tallgrass prairie, and a small wetland. The diversity of habitats makes this a favorite birding area for Wichita residents. During the winter large numbers of Harris' sparrows enliven the hedgerows. The wood duck boxes are taken over by screech-owls. Great horned owls and red-tailed hawks are commonly seen. Spring and fall migrations bring warblers and vireos. Summer is highlighted by indigo buntings, kingbirds, herons, and egrets. Nocturnal residents include raccoons, white-tailed deer, coyotes, and red foxes. A surprising number of hikers have seen mink playing and hunting along the stream. An inspection of the grassy areas will reveal the runways of cotton rats. These rodents support the many predators in the park. From the bridges over Chisholm Creek you can check partially submerged brush piles and logs for western painted turtles and Graham's crayfish snakes. Scheduled for completion in 1995, a nature center will provide a wide variety of educational opportunities. Wildlife displays, native fish aquariums, programs, and classes are just a few of the offerings planned by this multiagency facility operated by the Wichita Department of Parks and Recreation, Kansas Department of Wildlife and Parks, and U.S. Fish and Wildlife Service.

Directions: Chisholm Creek Park is located at 3238 North Oliver in northeast Wichita. The nature center will be located at the intersection of Woodlawn and 29th Street North. **Ownership:** City of Wichita (316-264-8323) **280 acres** 🅿 ⚥ H₂0 ☂ ⛺ 🚶

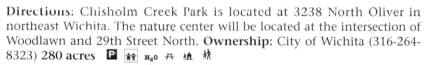

Calls from migrating flocks of Canada geese once symbolized the wilderness. Lakes and reservoirs attract them, but these adaptable birds are becoming urban residents as well.

57 Wichita Rivers

There are more wild animals than people in Wichita! It's one of the best places in Kansas for close viewing of large flocks of Canada geese. Over 8,000 geese arrive in fall; the best viewing occurs between late November and early March. The geese are outstanding subjects for wildlife photographers. The best viewing areas are along the Big Arkansas River north of Pawnee Street and on the Little Arkansas River along Oak Park and Central Riverside Park. Oak Park, noted for its dense woodlands, is also a great birding area during the spring migration. Mississippi kites nest here annually. At Central Riverside Park, be sure to visit the Kansas Wildlife Exhibit, which features beavers, red foxes, porcupines, hawks, owls, turtles, and other native animals. The many water bodies in Wichita also attract one of the largest heron populations in the state. Eight species of herons are found in the city. From late April through September, great egrets, snowy egrets, and little blue herons are often seen fishing along the rivers. A couple of good spots to watch for them are in the Big Arkansas River north of Pawnee Street and in the river adjacent to Old Cowtown Museum and Sim Park. Scan the wooded areas of Sim Park carefully—it is one of the most reliable spots to see the resident secretive red fox. The wooded areas of Sim Park and the adjacent grounds of Botanica also provide excellent opportunities to view birds and butterflies.

Directions: Begin your exploration of Wichita rivers at the intersection of Seneca Street and McLean Boulevard, near the confluence of the Big Arkansas River and the Little Arkansas River. Pawnee Street is reached by traveling 3 miles south on McLean Boulevard. To reach Central Riverside Park and Oak Park, go north from the intersection of Seneca Street and McLean Boulevard 1 block to Stackman Drive. Stackman Drive, which follows the curves of the Little Arkansas River into Central Riverside Park, turns into West River Boulevard; turn east at the 11th Street bridge to reach Oak Park. To reach Old Cowtown Museum, Botanica, and Sim Park, travel from the intersection of Seneca Street and McLean Boulevard, 1 block north to Stackman Drive. Follow Stackman another block northwest and then follow Sim Park Drive west to all three areas. **Ownership:** City of Wichita (316-264-8323) $\boxed{P}$ ⛹ H_2O ⛺ ⚲

> *Kansas is home to more than 700 species of vertebrates (animals with backbones). There are as many as 20,000 species of insects and other invertebrates. With these numbers, outdoor enthusiasts have endless opportunities for watching, studying, and enjoying wildlife.*

58 Pawnee Prairie Park

Pawnee Prairie Park in west Wichita is the largest natural area in the city. Over 400 acres of woodlands and prairie provide ideal viewing opportunities for a winter deer herd that usually numbers around 25. Wild turkeys have nested here, and some lucky visitors have seen red foxes, coyotes, and bobcats. Nearly 10 miles of trails along Cowskin Creek make exploration easy. These trails can be muddy following rain. While hiking, expect to see great horned owls, woodpeckers, Carolina wrens, and other woodland birds. Spring birding during the warbler migration can be excellent. The park has abundant beaver activity. The creek banks are dotted with tree stumps gnawed by foraging beavers. There are some dams, and slides indicate favorite travel routes. Muskrats and mink are occasionally seen. One of the best ways to learn which mammals are resident is by searching for tracks along the creek banks. Raccoons, opossums, and striped skunks are common. The area also provides critical habitat for the eastern spotted skunk, a Kansas threatened species.

Directions: Pawnee Prairie Park has two main entrances: the Nature Center entrance, at 2625 South Tyler Road, and the Picnic Area entrance, at 9910 West Pawnee. **Ownership:** City of Wichita (316-264-8323) **400 acres**

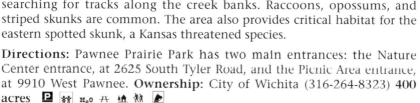

59 Lake Afton

Located near the largest city in the state, Lake Afton can be crowded with picnickers, campers, boaters, and swimmers. In spite of the people, the trees surrounding the lake are ideal for nesting eastern and western kingbirds, northern orioles, and American robins. Throughout the year great blue herons are commonly seen along the shoreline. In spring and fall observe migrating white pelicans. Ducks, Canada geese, and gulls are present through the winter. The 1-mile, self-guided nature trail takes hikers along a cattail marsh and mudflat that can be productive when water levels are just right. More than 60 stations on this trail highlight wildlife information and other features of the area. Watch for thirteen-lined ground squirrels, ornate box turtles, and bullfrogs along the edge of the water. Wildflowers are also abundant in the unmowed areas east of the access road on the east side of the lake. In early June as many as 50 species can be identified in a short walk. Of special interest is the Lake Afton Observatory open every Friday, Saturday, and Sunday evening. Share the excitement of the night sky through the observatory's 16-inch telescope.

Directions: Lake Afton is about 20 miles southwest of downtown Wichita on MacArthur Road at 247th Street West. It can also be reached from U.S. 54 by turning south at the Lake Afton sign at Viola Road 3 miles west of Goddard. Travel 3 miles south and 1 mile east to reach the lake. **Ownership:** Sedgwick County (316-794-2774) **720 acres**

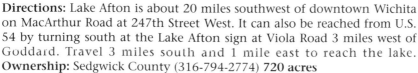

60 Cheney Reservoir

Around this reservoir, which was constructed primarily as a municipal water supply for the city of Wichita, both Cheney State Park and Cheney Wildlife Area have been developed. The west shore area of the state park contains grassy campsites under tall cottonwood trees, ideal for red-headed woodpeckers, orioles, kingbirds, and Mississippi kites. Scan the open water for large flocks of waterfowl during migrations and for bald eagles during the winter. Cheney Wildlife Area on the north end of the reservoir offers more diverse habitats and consequently more wildlife than the park. Trees, shrubs, native grasses, and forbs have been planted. This area supports pheasants, quail, rabbits, and squirrels. Deer are plentiful, and sometimes coyotes, raccoons, and black-tailed jackrabbits are seen. Most of the streams flowing through the area have abundant beaver sign. A Canada goose restoration flock has been established, and pairs are often found nesting during the spring. Where the Ninnescah River's north fork flows into the reservoir, watch for wood ducks, belted kingfishers, green-backed herons, and woodland birds. The shallow areas on the north end of the reservoir also attract large flocks of white pelicans during spring and fall migrations.

Directions: Cheney Reservoir is located approximately 14 miles south of Hutchinson on K-17 and approximately 30 miles west of Wichita. From U.S. 54 go 4 miles north on K-251 to the Cheney Reservoir dam. Pick up a lake map at the state park because the roads around the lake can be confusing. **Ownership:** USBuRec; KDWP; Cheney State Park (316-542-3664); Cheney Wildlife Area (316-459-6922) **16,700 acres** 🅿 🚻 H₂0 🌲 ⛺ 🚶 ⛴

Nature photography is one of Kansans' most popular outdoor activities. The availability of home video cameras has enhanced this interest.

61 Byron Walker Wildlife Area

Biodiversity at its best! One of the premier wildlife spots in the state, this site was named for its long-time manager. It has streamside woodlands, native prairies, food plots, shrub plantings, several ponds, a state lake, developed wetland, and 8 miles of the South Fork Ninnescah River. Birders, photographers, and other wildlife enthusiasts will find many opportunities to see wildlife. A small herd of bison can be easily seen just east of the headquarters at the U.S. 54 rest area. West of the bison pen, 3.4 miles, an entry leads south into a scenic portion of the wildlife area. The rolling sand prairie has abundant thickets of sandhill plums. Watch for pheasants, quail, doves, meadowlarks, grasshopper sparrows, and other prairie birds. Running through much of the area is the South Fork Ninnescah River. The sandy-bottomed river runs shallow and clear. Watch for belted kingfishers and herons outfishing the anglers! Deer are abundant and a wild turkey population is well established. Kingman State Lake is popular for fishing and camping. The woods around the lake support many nesting birds, including Mississippi kites, orioles, kingbirds, robins, and indigo buntings. Eastern bluebirds nest in boxes provided for them. During migrations, warblers, vireos, and flycatchers are abundant. A good way to view the wildlife is to hike the trail beginning at the northeast corner of the lake. The resident raccoons, beaver, muskrats, deer, and bobcats are very secretive, but watch for tracks and other signs. A marsh on the west side of the lake is home to mallards, teal, and nesting wood ducks. While hiking the dikes be alert for rails, grebes, herons, and cormorants, as well as reptiles and amphibians. Painted turtles, sliders, and northern water snakes often bask in the sun. At the water's edge watch for bullfrogs, plains leopard frogs, and tiny cricket frogs. The Great Plains toad and Woodhouse's toad, two favorites of kids, are abundant.

Directions: Byron Walker Wildlife Area is located 7 miles west of Kingman on U.S. 54. **Ownership:** KDWP (316-532-3242) **4,530 acres**

Kansas has ample numbers of lakes and streams along with some excellent wetland habitats to attract waterfowl such as this drake mallard.

Mike Blair

62 Pratt Fish Hatchery

This is a wonderful place to learn about many kinds of Kansas wildlife. The Operations Office of the Kansas Department of Wildlife and Parks is located near Pratt along the South Fork Ninnescah River. Visitors to the Pratt Conservation Education Center (open seven days a week from April through Labor Day) can see displays about predators, shorebirds, waterfowl, eggs, reptiles, and amphibians. There are also 12 aquariums featuring native fish. A nature trail and interpreted wildlife habitats are being developed. The education center is surrounded by the Pratt Fish Hatchery—covering 187 acres and consisting of 87 ponds. Channel catfish, largemouth bass, striped bass, walleye, sauger, and bluegill are produced here. During spring and fall migrations, many species of shorebirds use ponds in varying stages of drawdowns. Terns and gulls are common during these times; occasionally an osprey can be seen. In the warmer seasons, herons, kingfishers, and sunning turtles are visible around the hatchery ponds. Park at the office and walk along some of the ponds on the east side to get a good view. To see the south side of the main battery of ponds, drive west on K-64 toward Pratt. Carefully pull off to the side of the road as traffic is regular. About 1,000 Canada geese usually overwinter in the area and about 50 are produced yearly from nesting platforms on some of the rearing ponds. Pratt County Veterans Memorial Lake lies immediately east of the hatchery and office. The lake attracts ducks, herons, and kingfishers, and the extensive cattail marsh at the west end is alive with red-winged blackbirds and wading birds in the summer. The South Fork Ninnescah River flows along the north side of the hatchery and lake. Beaver activity is visible in many places along this scenic stream. During the evenings, watch for deer in adjacent fields.

Directions: Pratt Fish Hatchery is 2 miles east and 1 mile south of Pratt on K-64. Pratt County Lake is reached by traveling east on the road south of the hatchery and operations office. **Ownership:** KDWP (316-672-5911) **200 acres** 🅿 ⛹ H₂0 🏕 ⒶⓀ 🚤 ⊗

Huge flocks of circling white pelicans and sandhill cranes are seasonal highlights at Quivira National Wildlife Refuge and Cheyenne Bottoms.

63 Quivira National Wildlife Refuge

First-time visitors to this refuge are surprised to discover the abundance and diversity of wildlife. The bird checklist documents over 270 species. Mammals are also abundant: white-tailed deer, raccoons, badgers, bobcats, coyotes, and black-tailed prairie dogs. Wild turkeys find food and cover along the shelter belts. Waterfowl may reach over 100,000 in the fall and 300,000 in the spring. Look for white pelicans, sandhill cranes, greater and lesser yellowlegs, long-billed dowitchers, black-necked stilts, and several species of sandpipers. Occasionally in the spring, endangered whooping cranes stop for a visit. Nesting birds include 11 species of waterfowl as well as American avocets, least terns, and snowy plovers. Summer raptors include Swainson's hawks, Mississippi kites, northern harriers, and red-tailed hawks. Bald eagles and golden eagles winter on the refuge. Little Salt Marsh, north of the refuge headquarters, is a good place to see waterfowl, grebes, and herons. The best views, however, are along the wildlife drive at the north end of the refuge in Big Salt Marsh. The one-way gravel road takes visitors through the marshes and along the cat-tail-bordered lakes. American bitterns and yellow-headed blackbirds can often be photographed at close range from your vehicle. This is a great place to see water turtles and a number of kinds of lizards and snakes. Massasauga rattlesnakes like to sun on the roads in the warmer seasons.

Directions: From Stafford, travel east 6 miles on U.S. 50 to Zenith. Turn north at Zenith and travel 8 miles to the refuge headquarters. Stop here to pick up a map and bird checklist. **Ownership:** USFWS (316-486-2393) 21,820 acres

Visitors to Kansas' central wetland complex of Cheyenne Bottoms and Quivira will be rewarded with sights like this. In good years Cheyenne Bottoms Wildlife Area will attract over half a million waterfowl.

Mike Blair

64 Cheyenne Bottoms Wildlife Area

Don't miss this one! Cheyenne Bottoms is a natural depression of about 60 square miles lying north of the Arkansas River in the center of the state. It is the largest marsh in the interior of the United States and has been designated a Wetland of International Importance. The area is considered the most important shorebird migration point in the western hemisphere. Approximately 45 percent of the North American shorebird population stops at the Bottoms during spring migration. Although known primarily for birds, the area also contains raccoons, deer, beavers, muskrats, and mink as well as a variety of reptiles. Western painted turtles, sliders, diamondback and northern water snakes, and Graham's crayfish snakes frequent the water's edge. In spring and fall, massasauga rattlesnakes regularly bask in the sun on the road. Visitors to Cheyenne Bottoms should stop at information stations for maps, checklists, and a driving tour booklet. By following the tour, visitors get a better understanding of the significance of the area as well as the complexity of managing a wetland resource with limited water. In times of severe drought, the Bottoms may go completely dry. At least 320 species of birds have been recorded at the Bottoms. The area is critical habitat for several threatened and endangered species, including the whooping crane, bald eagle, peregrine falcon, least tern, and piping plover. More than 25 species of ducks and geese have been identified at the Bottoms and at times have numbered in excess of 600,000 birds. In mid-March thousands of sandhill cranes stop on the way to their staging area along the Platte River in Nebraska. April brings tens of thousands of shorebirds to the mudflats where they probe the mud for bloodworms, the larval stage of a small fly known as the midge. During the summer, swarms of these insects are seen over the marshes. Common shorebirds include a variety of sandpipers, plovers, phalaropes, avocets, godwits, and dowitchers. Summer visitors often encounter huge flocks of red-winged and yellow-headed blackbirds. Herons are also common during the summer; great blue herons, snowy egrets, black-crowned night herons, and American bitterns search the shallows for fish and frogs. A highlight of fall migration is the impressive flocks of undulating, circling, white pelicans. At times, large "islands" of the birds are seen across the marsh. All wildlife watchers should make an annual pilgrimage to Cheyenne Bottoms—the most important ecosystem in Kansas.

Directions: From U.S. 56, east of Great Bend, travel 6 miles northeast on K-156 to one of two entrances to Cheyenne Bottoms Wildlife Area. To use the other entrance, drive 6 miles north of Great Bend on U.S. 281 and 2 miles east to the area headquarters. Visitors can drive on approximately 15 miles of gravel roads within the area. **Ownership:** KDWP (316-793-7730) **20,000 acres** 🅿 ⛺ ⚐ ⚉

Northcentral

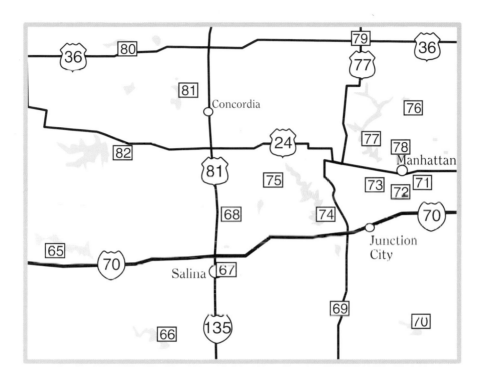

65 Wilson Reservoir

Beautifully clear Wilson Reservoir graces the rolling grasslands of Post Rock Country. The Saline River, open waters of the reservoir, numerous streams, marshes, riparian woodlands, and upland mixedgrass prairie provide the diversity for wildlife. To become familiar with the area, take a walk on Bur Oak Nature Trail in Sylvan Park below the dam. The river below the outlet has beaver dams and cone-shaped muskrat dens. Rocktown Natural Area, a registered Kansas natural and scientific area in Lucas Park west of the dam, is a good place to view massive red Dakota sandstone formations, prairie grasses, wildflowers, and birds. The grasslands around the lake are good areas to look for mule deer, coyotes, greater prairie chickens, and ring-necked pheasants. Woody and brushy tracts near milo fields attract white-tailed deer and northern bobwhite quail. Thirteen-lined ground squirrels and pocket gopher mounds are common in the campgrounds. On summer nights Ord's kangaroo rats can be seen on sandy backroads in the beam of headlights. Reptile lovers should examine rocky areas for collared lizards, sandy sites for six-lined racerunners, and marshes and wet meadows for common and plains garter snakes. Bullsnakes, the farmer's friend, are abundant in many different habitats. Birders find rock wrens, chimney swifts, western kingbirds, northern mockingbirds, and loggerhead shrikes in the summer. Hundreds of cliff-swallow nests can be found under Hell Creek Bridge at the Wilson Otoe Area. In fall and spring, orange-crowned, yellow, and yellow-rumped warblers inhabit the woodlands. The lake attracts migrating ducks, grebes, cormorants, and geese; sometimes you can see ospreys and sandhill cranes. Winter attractions include mountain bluebirds and golden and bald eagles. The Kansas Department of Wildlife and Parks has reintroduced young golden eagles in hopes of establishing some nesting pairs. Walk the Dakota Trail in the Hell Creek area of the state park to see many of the region's grasses and wildflowers.

Directions: The dam is 8 miles north of the Wilson exit (206) on I-70. For a lake map, guide to Bur Oak Trail, and checklists, go to the Corps of Engineers Information Center below the dam. Park permits, a wildlife area map, and Dakota Trail guide are available at the Wilson State Park office south of the dam. For a magnificent drive through the Dakota and Greenhorn (Post Rock) geological formations, take Southshore Drive from Wilson State Park to Bunker Hill. **Ownership:** USACE (913-658-2551); KDWP (913-658-2465) 18,086 acres 🅿 ♙ H₂0 ⊼ ☕ ☖ ☖ ⊛ ➳

During some winters as many as 50 bald eagles gather along the causeway near Wakefield at Milford Reservoir.

Occasionally seen in western Kansas, the golden eagle ranges up to 35 square miles in search of jackrabbits, cottontails, rodents, and snakes.

66 Kanopolis Reservoir

The Smoky Hill River valley in the Dakota Hills is the scenic backdrop for Kanopolis Reservoir. Hundreds of migrating waterfowl can be seen in spring and fall. Look for geese, mergansers, pintails, wigeons, shovelers, teal, mallards, gadwalls, buffleheads, and goldeneyes. Prairie wildflowers such as purple poppy mallow, prairie spiderwort, yucca, prairie wild rose, butterfly milkweed, and blue false indigo, along with little bluestem and sideoats grama grasses are only a few of the 423 species of plants that can be found along the Buffalo Track Canyon Nature Trail. Watch for collared lizards, Texas horned lizards, six-lined racerunners, Great Plains skinks, and other reptiles. In grassland areas, prairie dogs, mule deer, horned larks, meadowlarks, and kingbirds are common. There are signs of beaver and raccoon along waterways. In open woodlands and croplands watch for white-tailed deer, pheasants, bobwhite quail, and coyotes. In winter, bald eagles are commonly seen flying over the lake, and turkey vultures can be seen in summer.

Directions: From I-135 in Salina, take K-140 about 21 miles west to K-141. Travel approximately 9 miles south to the state park office in the Horsethief Canyon area north of the dam. To get to the Corps of Engineers Information Center, which features exhibits on the area's archaeology, history, and natural resources, drive to the south side of the dam, then take the east road. Be sure to pick up a Kanopolis Legacy Lake Trail guide and tour 27 sites in the area, including Mushroom Park Area. **Ownership:** USACE (913-546-2294); KDWP (913-546-2565) **18,000 acres** P ⚌ H₂0 ⊼ Ⓒ ⚇ ⚇ ▶ ⊜ ⇋

Mike Blair

67 Lakewood Park Natural Area and Kansas Fishes Exhibit

Lakewood Park in Salina provides an opportunity to explore an urban nature area. Hiking trails weave through an area containing prairie, woodlands, and water. The entire site is developed around an old sand quarry, which is now dedicated to nature interpretation and recreation. Many species of wildlife typical of urban woodlands are found here, including white-tailed deer, fox squirrels, and raccoons. Several nest boxes and houses have been erected to attract bats, screech-owls, purple martins, eastern bluebirds, and wrens. Visitors to the Headquarters Lodge can enjoy the activity around the bird feeders or search for insects in the butterfly garden. Plant enthusiasts can find over 35 species, and a small native prairie blooms with butterfly milkweed, purple prairie clover, lead plant, and coneflower. While in Salina, visit the Kansas Fishes Exhibit in Central Mall. The 15,000-gallon aquarium (25 feet long, 12 feet wide, and 6.5 feet deep) recreates a typical Kansas river habitat complete with native fishes, including channel catfish, bluegill, crappie, bass, and walleye.

Directions: Lakewood Park, in northeast Salina, is east of Ohio Street between North Street and Iron Street. The Kansas Fishes Exhibit is in Central Mall at 2259 South 9th Street. **Ownership:** City of Salina (913-823-1245); Central Mall Merchants Association (913-825-7733) **99 acres**

P ♀♂ H₂O ⅋ ⚿ 🚶 🚲

Commonly called the "zebra minnow," the hardy plains killifish can be found in the shallow, salty, sand-bottomed streams of western Kansas.

Ken Brunson

68 Ottawa State Fishing Lake

Ottawa State Fishing Lake is located on Sand Creek in the Smoky Hills. Tall-grass prairie and croplands surround the cottonwood and hackberry woodlands that border the lake and the two streams that feed it. Look for white-tailed deer and coyotes year-round. From spring through fall, sliders and painted turtles can be seen basking on snags and rocks near the low-water bridge at the north end of the lake. American goldfinches, black-capped chickadees, and northern cardinals are active at the edges of the timber and thickets. Signs of beavers, raccoons, and muskrats are evident along the streams and marshy areas of the lake. Watch for wood ducks, mallards, belted kingfishers, and wading great blue herons. A few miles west, in an area of cedar trees and bluestem grasses overlooking the Solomon River valley, mysteriously loom nearly 200 huge spheres of Dakota sandstone. These rare concretions, ranging up to 27 feet in diameter, have been designated a National Natural Landmark. A visit to this Rock City, owned by the city of Minneapolis, is well worth your time. There is an entry fee.

Directions: Ottawa State Fishing Lake is southeast of Minneapolis, 4 miles east of U.S. 81 on K-93. Rock City is 2.5 miles southwest of Minneapolis on K-106. **Ownership:** KDWP (913-658-2465) **711 acres**

69 Herington City Lakes

These two Flint Hills lakes—Lake Herington and Herington Reservoir—are just west of Herington. The shallow south end of Lake Herington has an extensive cattail marsh with several snags. Herington Reservoir has an abundance of standing timber also in its shallow end. The surrounding land comprises native tallgrass prairie and cropland. Best viewing is during spring and fall migrations. Ducks to watch for include redhead, lesser scaup, mallard, green-winged teal, common goldeneye, and bufflehead. Migrating yellow-headed blackbirds and pelicans frequently stop over. Sandpipers and plovers can be seen on the mudflats. During spring and fall, ospreys fish the waters. Great blue herons are seen in the shallows, and double-crested cormorants are frequently sighted on the snags and standing timbers. Look for red-winged blackbirds in the cattails. Mourning doves, scissor-tailed flycatchers, eastern meadowlarks, dickcissels, and grasshopper sparrows are common in the grasslands. Wild turkeys, white-tailed deer, opossums, and raccoons are often seen at dusk and dawn.

Directions: From the four-way stop at the junction of U.S. 77 and U.S. 56, travel 1 mile west on U.S. 56 (Trapp Street) to 5th Street, then 0.2 miles north to Walnut Street. Take Walnut east 1 mile, then follow the paved road southwest 1.4 miles to Lake Herington. Herington Reservoir is 1 mile farther west. **Ownership:** City of Herington (913-258-2271; 913-258-3051) **1,600 acres**

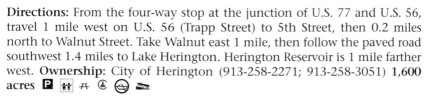

70 Council Grove Reservoir

Scenic Council Grove Reservoir has a rocky shoreline and an abundance of picnic, camping, boating, and hiking areas. During spring and fall, the reservoir attracts flocks of migrating ducks, geese, cormorants, and gulls. In winter bald eagles are frequently seen perched in the trees surrounding the lake. The Canada geese are quite tame and often allow vehicles to approach. The Canning Creek Cove area has a trail of eastern bluebird nest boxes along the entrance drive. Watch for the bluebirds in the spring. Hikers may also wish to explore the 2.2-mile Tallgrass Day Trail, originating at the campground entrance. The shady picnic and campground areas have nesting robins, kingbirds, and orioles. Bat houses have been erected here and at several other places around the lake. To look for wildlife in a different habitat visit the Council Grove Wildlife Area along Munkers Creek. Watch for deer and squirrels. The narrow, wooded lane also provides visitors the opportunity to view winter sparrows, towhees, cardinals, and woodpeckers from the comfort of a car. Visitors with high-clearance vehicles can use the low-water bridge to position themselves in the middle of the creek and look upstream and downstream for wood ducks, kingfishers, and green-backed herons. During spring migration the woods along this creek may be alive with warblers, vireos, flycatchers, and other songbirds.

Directions: From Council Grove, go 1.8 miles north on K-177 from the intersection of U.S. 56. From this intersection, Canning Creek Cove area is 3.2 miles west across the dam. To visit Council Grove Wildlife Area, continue north on K-177 another 3.7 miles and exit to the east. **Ownership:** USACE (316-767-5195); KDWP (316-767-5900) **5,975 acres** 🅿 👪 H₂0 🎋 ⓐ 🚶 ⛵

71 Pillsbury Crossing Wildlife Area

At this spot Deep Creek flows over a limestone ledge and forms a waterfall with a drop of about 4 feet. Just upstream, about 100 feet of the road crosses the ledge and vehicles travel through several inches of water. (Be careful—during high water this road is not passable!) This is a pleasant picnic spot, and the kids will enjoy wading in the rock-bottomed creek. Beaver activity is visible on the trees, and wood ducks are sometimes seen. The riparian woodlands also attract a variety of birds and many squirrels. A great blue heron rookery is located a short distance away (you'll need binoculars or spotting scopes). The birds usually occupy the nests by mid-March. Remember, this is private property and the birds are easily disturbed. Please view them from the road.

Directions: From the bridge over the Kansas River at the south edge of Manhattan, travel 1.7 miles southeast on K-177 to Riley County 911. Travel east 3.9 miles to an intersection that is easily missed as the road bends south. Exit on Pillsbury Crossing Road and go another 2.3 miles east to Pillsbury Crossing Wildlife Area. To reach the heron rookery, return to Riley County 911 and head south for 1.5 miles. The pavement turns into a rock road and passes the Deep Creek Schoolhouse. The colony is visible in the large sycamore trees in the creek bottom to the east. **Ownership:** KDWP (913-539-7941) **59 acres** 🅿 👪 🎋 ⓐ

Gere Brehm

In spring and early fall the rapid "sweet, sweet, sweet, I'm so sweet" call of the yellow warbler can be heard in streamside woodlands of cottonwood and willow.

72 Konza Prairie

Most of Konza was once a part of Dewey Cattle Ranch. In the 1970s, the Nature Conservancy purchased the property, over 13 square miles; it is managed by Kansas State University to be used as a research natural area. Because many research projects are currently in progress, most of the area is closed to the public. A public nature trail, however, takes visitors on a scenic hike across the virgin tallgrass prairie and atop the limestone-capped hills overlooking Dewey ranch. Brochures and trail guides are found at the trailhead. The trail crosses Kings Creek with a forest community of oak, walnut, hickory, and hackberry trees. Look for woodpecker holes, which are also used by nesting eastern bluebirds, tufted titmice, and black-capped chickadees. Deer tracks are abundant, but the deer are most commonly seen early in the morning or in late evening. Limestone outcrops characterize the Konza Prairie landscape. The shrub community is an important habitat for Bell's vireos, collared lizards, and eastern wood rats. The wood rat's huge stick nest is often found at the base of large rocks. The dominant plants of the tallgrass prairie are grasses. Big bluestem, Indiangrass, little bluestem, and switchgrass are the most abundant. During spring and summer the prairie is a canvas of colorful wildflowers! Prairie birds include upland sandpipers, eastern meadowlarks, mourning doves, and grasshopper sparrows. In spring, those who hike to the far end of Research Unit K20A, about 6 miles round-trip, may find greater prairie chickens and Henslow's sparrows. Watch for the sparrows singing from the tallest plants in the upper levels of the watershed.

Directions: Konza Prairie is south of Manhattan. Travel 6.3 miles south of K-177 on McDowell Creek Road along the east side of the Kansas River. The area can also be reached from I-70 by taking Exit 307 and traveling north 4.9 miles on McDowell Creek Road (also identified as Riley County 901). **Ownership:** Nature Conservancy; Kansas State University (913-539-1961) **8,600 acres** P 🚶

73 Fort Riley Military Reservation

Fort Riley offers most of the wildlife species found in northcentral Kansas, including at least one—the wapiti, or elk—not otherwise found free-ranging in most of the state. Approximately 50 elk roam the reservation—they are usually in the northern sector. Visitors should know that some restrictions have been established to ensure travel safety and the fort's primary mission of military training. For information on current regulations and elk-viewing or fall bugling locations, call the Fish and Wildlife Administrator at the Natural Resources Office (number listed below). The First Territorial Capitol Museum is located at Fort Riley and the adjacent Kaw River Nature Trail provides good wildlife viewing. The trail, a little over 1 mile long, takes hikers into the woodlands along the Kansas River. The dominant trees include cottonwood, green ash, and box elder with an understory of gooseberry, grape, and Virginia creeper. Common mammals of the area include raccoons, opossums, striped skunks, coyotes, fox squirrels, deer, beavers, muskrats, and eastern wood rats. Five-lined skinks, common garter snakes, and rat snakes are here along with several species of frogs, toads, and aquatic turtles. The woodlands contain a variety of woodpeckers and songbirds. During winter, bald eagles may be seen flying along the river or perched in large cottonwoods that provide them a good view.

Directions: Fort Riley Military Reservation is located between Junction City and Manhattan. From Manhattan, take K-18 west 8 miles. Travel through the town of Ogden. The Natural Resources Office is a little over 2 miles west of Ogden; the First Territorial Capitol Museum and the Kaw River Nature Trail are another mile west of the resources office. **Ownership:** U.S. Department of the Army (913-239-6211) **101,000 acres** P ♀♂ H₂0 ⚲ ♀♂

One of the state's most common turtles, painted turtles are easily recognized by their colorful undersides. Look for them sunning themselves on logs or rocks along the shoreline.

74 Milford Reservoir

The Milford Reservoir region contains several areas of interest for wildlife watchers. (The northern end of the reservoir is discussed in site 75.) The entire reservoir plays host to a variety of aquatic birds. They can be observed from Milford State Park, Milford Wildlife Area, the reservoir dam, or any of the numerous access points. Great blue herons are most visible in the summer. Spring and fall migrations bring the largest numbers of ducks, geese, pelicans, and ospreys. During winter, bald eagles and some waterfowl are always present. The dam provides a good vantage point for scanning the area. Below the dam are Milford Nature Center and Milford Fish Hatchery. Tours are available by appointment only. Beginning just south of the nature center is the Tallgrass Nature Trail. A backyard habitat demonstration area features seasonal songbirds and butterflies. While hiking the trail, watch for beaver, wood ducks, pheasants, quail, herons, kingfishers, and during the summer, numerous six-lined racerunner lizards. The nature center and hatchery are open Monday through Friday, 10 A.M. to 4 P.M. From April through October, the weekend hours are from noon to 4 P.M. Programs and tours can be scheduled by calling 913-238-5323.

Directions: Milford Reservoir, near Junction City, is 5 miles north of I-70 (Exit 295) and 2 miles west on K-57. Milford Nature Center and Milford Fish Hatchery are located below the dam. Maps can be obtained at the information center at the south end of the dam. **Ownership:** USACE (913-238-5714); KDWP (913-238-5323, Nature Center; 913-238-3014, State Park) 37,000 acres �P 👥 H₂0 🏕 Ⓐ 🏛 🚶 🚤 ⊕

75 Kansas Landscape Arboretum

Kansas Landscape Arboretum lies just south of Wakefield on the west side of Milford Reservoir. Over 1,000 species of native and exotic woody plants adapted to the Kansas environment are found here. The gates are open daily from 8 A.M. to dusk, March 1 to October 31. Much of the area is left in native vegetation, and foot trails provide easy access to both prairie and woodland habitats. Although the area is managed for plant life, wildlife can also be found. Deer are often spooked from the wooded areas during the middle of the day. The woods attract Harris' sparrows, northern cardinals, blue jays, and several species of woodpeckers. Nest boxes for eastern bluebirds have been erected to enhance viewing opportunities. From the arboretum, Milford Reservoir is visible to the east. The causeway over the north end of the reservoir, just east of Wakefield, is one of the area's best sites for wildlife viewing. Clay County Park, on the west end of the causeway, is a good place to park while scanning the area for birds. In winter, as many as 50 bald eagles have been seen. Flocks of white pelicans are common during spring and fall. Ducks, geese, cormorants, grebes, herons, gulls, and shorebirds are also abundant during migrations.

Directions: From K-82 in Wakefield, turn south on Dogwood Street and follow the signs just short of 1 mile to Kansas Landscape Arboretum. Clay County Park lies on the east edge of Wakefield just west of the bridge over Milford Reservoir. **Ownership:** Kansas Landscape Arboretum, Inc. (913-461-5760) **193 acres** ▢ 🚶 👥

76 Pottawatomie State Fishing Lake No. 1

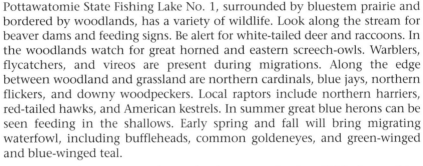

Pottawatomie State Fishing Lake No. 1, surrounded by bluestem prairie and bordered by woodlands, has a variety of wildlife. Look along the stream for beaver dams and feeding signs. Be alert for white-tailed deer and raccoons. In the woodlands watch for great horned and eastern screech-owls. Warblers, flycatchers, and vireos are present during migrations. Along the edge between woodland and grassland are northern cardinals, blue jays, northern flickers, and downy woodpeckers. Local raptors include northern harriers, red-tailed hawks, and American kestrels. In summer great blue herons can be seen feeding in the shallows. Early spring and fall will bring migrating waterfowl, including buffleheads, common goldeneyes, and green-winged and blue-winged teal.

Directions: The lake is 5 miles north of Westmoreland on K-99. **Ownership:** KDWP (913-539-7941) **190 acres** P ♙ H$_2$O ⌂ Ⓐ ⊘ ⇌

Thousands of mountain bluebirds overwinter in the cedar-dotted Gypsum Hills near Medicine Lodge, while thousands of bats occupy the many hibernation caves nearby.

Bob Gress

Once greatly reduced in numbers, the population of eastern bluebirds has been boosted by the recent popularity of bluebird nest boxes. The birds eagerly accept the houses placed on fence posts bordering open pasturelands.

77 Tuttle Creek Reservoir

Tuttle Creek Reservoir lies in the Big Blue River valley just north of Manhattan, surrounded by the wooded valleys and tallgrass prairie uplands of the Flint Hills. At the northern end of the lake is the wildlife area, where migrating waterfowl and shorebirds can be seen in fall and spring. The best sites for viewing prairie wildlife are the Kansas State University Range Research Unit (2 miles southwest of the dam) and along Prairie Parkway (west of K-13), east of the lake. The most accessible and probably best all-around viewing area is River Pond State Park below the dam. Here along the river, gadwall and common goldeneye ducks along with common mergansers and ring-billed gulls are abundant in winter. On occasion oldsquaw ducks and common loons are sighted. In mid-winter bald eagles fish the river pond and perch on the tall trees of Eagle Island. East of the outlet channel, ponds support beaver and muskrats year-round and American wigeons and northern shovelers in winter. Listen for western chorus frogs in March and April and bullfrogs and cricket frogs in summer. During migrations, watch for warblers, sparrows, and ospreys. Herons are often seen in summer. In the grasslands along Prairie Parkway you can see upland sandpipers as well as loggerhead shrikes and western kingbirds perched on fence posts. Eastern meadowlarks, dickcissels, grasshopper sparrows, and mourning doves are also frequently seen. On the Range Research Unit, greater prairie chickens boom in the pre-dawn light of April and May. A couple of miles west of Stockdale Cove, on private land along Mill Creek, tall sycamores hold large stick nests of great blue herons.

Directions: Tuttle Creek Dam is 4.5 miles north of Manhattan on K-177. Stop at the Corps of Engineers Information Center, west of the dam, for a reservoir map and trail guides. Park permits and wildlife area maps are available at the Tuttle Creek State Park Office below the dam on the east side. **Ownership:** USACE (913-539-8511); KDWP (913-539-7941) **26,800 acres**

78 Pottawatomie State Fishing Lake No. 2

Pottawatomie State Fishing Lake No. 2 is situated in a heavily wooded valley surrounded by tallgrass prairie. Start your visit with a hike on the nature trail at the northeast end of the lake. White-tailed deer, wild turkeys, northern bobwhite quail, and coyotes are present year-round. Wood ducks and beavers inhabit the streams flowing into the lake. Muskrats, great blue herons, frogs, and water snakes can be observed in the marshes. In summer look on fence posts in the surrounding prairies for upland sandpipers. Watch also for eastern meadowlarks, grasshopper sparrows, and dickcissels. If you look along the wooded fence lines at the edge of the meadows, you may see loggerhead shrikes and blue grosbeaks. The woodlands are home to many species of warblers and sparrows during migrations and to eastern screech-owls and great horned owls throughout the year. Migrating ospreys will occasionally visit the lake. In winter common goldeneyes, common mergansers, gadwalls, and buffleheads can be seen.

Directions: From K-177 in Manhattan, take K-24 east 2.9 miles. Follow the signs 3.5 miles north and west to the lake. **Ownership:** KDWP (913-539-7941) **249 acres** 🅿 ⚐ H_2O ⛺ Ⓒ ⊖ ⛵

The distinctive curved neck of the great blue heron is easily seen as this wading bird glides over the water at dusk. This efficient angler is one of the most-watched wildlife species in Kansas.

Mike Blair

79 Marysville City Park

Here's something unique! When entering the city, visitors are greeted by large signs proclaiming Marysville the Black Squirrel City. About 50 percent of the city's population of fox squirrels are black. Some squirrels show black patterns intermixed with normal coloration. The black coloration (called melanism) is caused by an excess of the dark pigment melanin in the fur of the animals. In wildlife melanism occurs much less frequently than the more common albinism, or white coloration. The residents of Marysville are justly proud of their claim to one of nature's more interesting animals. Many people feed them at backyard stations. The animals can be found throughout the city, but for visitors the best spot may be around the bandstand in the city park. There are nest holes in the large oak trees, so if you don't see squirrels immediately, be patient.

Directions: Marysville City Park is located along U.S. 77 on the south side of town. **Ownership:** City of Marysville (913-562-5331) **5 acres**

P ♣♣ H₂0 ⊼ ⓐ

Most people are familiar with the reddish color of the fox squirrel. "Black" fox squirrels are one of nature's rarities.

Bob Gress

80 Lovewell Reservoir

Lovewell Reservoir is situated in the Chalk Hills region of the Smoky Hills. Chalk bluffs, oak-covered hillsides, and upland prairies characterize this scenic area. Migrating waterfowl and shorebirds are drawn to the lake and wetlands. For the best wildlife views, drive roads nearest the water or hike along the reservoir shoreline. Pick up a park permit and map at the Lovewell Unit Office. On the north side of the reservoir are areas of short-grasses inhabited by thirteen-lined ground squirrels and black-tailed prairie dogs. During migrations Montana Creek and other coves provide good viewing of shorebirds and waterfowl. Watch for black-billed magpies in the woody edge along the lake and streams. Bobwhite quail will be close to thickets. Ring-necked pheasants should be in the grasslands, croplands, and along the roads. In the evening and early morning watch for wild turkey, both white-tailed and mule deer, coyotes, opossums, and raccoons. Secretive bobcats are here also. The Oak Hill area is a good spot for songbirds. Scan the open waters and shallows for cormorants, white pelicans, gulls, and herons. Spring to fall, look for mourning doves, red-tailed hawks, and turkey vultures. Bald eagles are becoming more common at this reservoir every winter.

Directions: From the center of Mankato, take U.S. 36 east 5 miles to K-14. Travel 9 miles north to North Shore Road, 4 miles east, and 0.5 miles south to the Lovewell Unit Office in Lovewell State Park. **Ownership:** USBuRec (913-753-4444); KDWP (913-753-4971) **6,275 acres**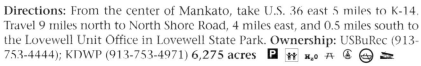

81 Jamestown Wildlife Area

This complex wetland is alive with many sights, sounds, and smells. Dams and dikes on Marsh Creek produced two large, shallow lakes with cattail marshes, an ideal place for migrating waterfowl and shorebirds. The best viewing seasons are from mid-February into May and from late August through November. The two best viewing sites are at the bridge between the lakes 0.5 miles west of the information area near the north dam and on the K-148 bridge over Marsh Creek. The south lake has a road bordering its east shore that is also an excellent viewing area. Common ducks include red-heads, ring-necked ducks, lesser scaup, mallards, green-winged teal, American wigeons, northern pintails, northern shovelers, blue-winged teal, ruddy ducks, common goldeneyes, buffleheads, and common mergansers. Greater white-fronted, snow, and Canada geese are also common. Other water birds include herons, avocets, terns, sandpipers, plovers, kingfishers, cormorants, and white pelicans. Look for the domed huts of the muskrats that thrive among the stands of cattails. With patience, you will eventually catch a glimpse of these water-loving mammals. Water turtles are plentiful.

Directions: From Concordia, take U.S. 81 north 8 miles to K-148. Go 10.5 miles on K-148 to Kackley and continue another 2 miles west to Courtland Road. Drive south 2.5 miles to the information and restroom area on the east side between the lakes. For further directions, use the map on the information board or contact the Lovewell Unit Office. For a map and checklist, contact Kansas Department of Wildlife and Parks, RR 2, Box 54A, Pratt KS 67124 **Ownership:** KDWP (913-753-4971) **3,230 acres**

82 Glen Elder Reservoir

Glen Elder Reservoir, the third largest reservoir in Kansas, lies at the confluence of the North and South forks of the Solomon River. The reservoir, known locally as Waconda Lake, covers Waconda Springs, a site sacred to generations of Plains Indians. The best times to visit are during the spring and fall migration seasons, when thousands of birds stop in the area. You can expect to see huge numbers of mallard ducks and Canada geese. Watch for redhead, lesser scaup, green-winged and blue-winged teal, common goldeneye, and bufflehead. The best views are from the dam and the north end of the causeway near the goose refuge. On the North Fork of the Solomon River, a riparian woodland of cottonwood, elm, oak, and hickory supports many songbirds. Watch for wood ducks among the dead trees standing in the water. In winter, scan the tall trees near the lakeshore and along the rivers for bald eagles. Common loons may be present during this season. Red-tailed hawks are frequently sighted throughout the year. Ring-necked pheasant, greater prairie chicken, and mule deer inhabit the grasslands and croplands. In the bottomlands, watch for white-tailed deer, wild turkeys, beaver, and raccoons. Listen for great horned owls and coyotes at night. If you visit from late spring to early fall, be sure to walk the Waconda Nature Trail in the park.

Directions: At the Glen Elder State Park Office, 1 mile west of Glen Elder on K-24, you can pick up a park permit, map, and trail guide. **Ownership:** USBuRec (913-545-3314); KDWP (913-545-3345) **12,600 acres**

$ P ⚥ H₂0 ⌇ Ⓐ ⊖ ⇒

Mike Blair

Kids are fascinated by the Texas horned lizard. But since these reptiles eat primarily ants, they are difficult to keep and should be returned to the wild after close encounters.

Northwest

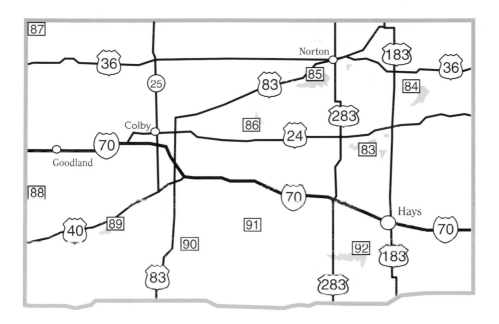

83 Webster Reservoir

84 Kirwin National Wildlife Refuge

85 Prairie Dog State Park

86 Antelope Lake

87 Arikaree Breaks Wildlife Drive

88 Mount Sunflower

89 Scott State Park

90 Chalk Pyramids

91 Castle Rock Drive

92 Cedar Bluff Reservoir

83 Webster Reservoir

Webster Reservoir, west of Stockton on the South Fork of the Solomon River, complements the picturesque Chalk Hills. The area's mixedgrass prairie, river, lake, marshes, and riparian trees and shrubs teem with wildlife. At the Webster State Park Office obtain a guide for the nature trail that leads through the grasslands and river woodlands west of the camping area. Spring through fall, inspect the grasslands along the trail for wildflowers, mourning doves, American kestrels, red-tailed hawks, and western meadowlarks. The riverside woodlands contain downy, red-bellied, and red-headed woodpeckers, blue jays, robins, orchard orioles, common yellowthroats, and black-billed magpies. Inspect spaces between the rocks for nests of eastern wood rats. At the bridge, green-backed and great blue herons and painted turtles are frequently seen. Tracks of raccoon and mink and gnawings of beaver should be evident along the bank. In summer, big brown bats live in colonies in the limestone cliffs along the trail. You'll probably see bank swallows here. Webster Wildlife Area extends west along both sides of the river for several miles. The grasslands and food plots here are ideal for mule deer, coyotes, ring-necked pheasants, bullsnakes, and western hognose snakes. The woodlands are inhabited by white-tailed deer, fox squirrels, wild turkeys, and northern bobwhite quail. During early summer nights, especially after heavy rains, the bleating trill of the Great Plains toad will command your attention. Spring and fall bring migrating white pelicans, waterfowl, and shorebirds to the lake. From late fall to early spring watch for Canada geese, snow geese, and bald eagles. In winter you can fish the stilling basin below the dam for rainbow trout. While in the area, another good wildlife site to visit is Rooks State Fishing Lake. Be on the lookout for sharks' teeth and other fossils among the chalk rocks and gravel of both areas.

Directions: To reach the Webster State Park office, go 8 miles west of Stockton on U.S. 24; then follow the signs southwest for 2.5 miles. At the office, pick up a park permit, maps, and trail guides. To reach Rooks State Fishing Lake, travel 0.5 miles south of Stockton on U.S. 183, then a little over 1 mile west. **Ownership:** USBuRec (913-839-4326); KDWP (913-425-6775) 10,380 acres **P** 🚻 H₂0 ⛱ Ⓐ 🏃 👣 ♿ ⚓

Kirwin National Wildlife Refuge is the winter home for thousands of Canada geese.

84 Kirwin National Wildlife Refuge

Here you can see lots of deer and geese! Located in the Smoky Hills, U-shaped Kirwin Reservoir is formed by Bow Creek and the North Fork of the Solomon River. Kirwin National Wildlife Refuge, established in 1954, is the first federal sanctuary authorized in Kansas. The refuge of nearly 11,000 acres is in the Central Flyway and one of the last major feeding stops for waterfowl migrating between wintering areas to the south and their northern breeding grounds. It includes the lake, riparian woodlands, nearly 4,000 acres of mixedgrass prairie, and about 2,000 acres of cultivated land, which provides nearly 20,000 bushels of corn and milo every year to migrating birds and other wildlife. Management practices also include green winter wheat browse for wintering geese, controlled burning, and short-term intensive grazing to maintain the grasslands. At Dog Town look for black-tailed prairie dogs, thirteen-lined ground squirrels, black-tailed jackrabbits, mule deer, horned larks, kingbirds, meadowlarks, kestrels, and red-tailed hawks. Double-crested cormorants and great blue herons nest on the lake. Yellow-headed blackbirds frequent marsh areas, and black-billed magpies forage in the open woodlands. Walk quietly on the nature trail and you may see wild turkey, white-tailed deer, and in summer, a variety of butterflies. Any time of year drive slowly in the evenings and early mornings along the roads north of the lake and you will see an amazing number of deer. Migrations bring thousands of shorebirds, wading birds, geese, ducks, white pelicans, and Franklin's gulls to the lake. Winter brings rough-legged hawks, golden and bald eagles, and thousands of mallards and Canada geese.

Directions: To reach the refuge office, go 6 miles east of Glade on K-9, then 1 mile south on the county road. Maps and checklists are available. **Ownership:** USFWS (913-543-6673) **10,778 acres** P 👫 H₂0 🏕 🅰 👫 ⚓

An accomplished digger, the great plains toad hides underground during summer days and emerges at night to feed on beetles and other insects. The bleating calls of the males at close range can be deafening.

87

85 Prairie Dog State Park

Prairie Dog State Park and Norton Wildlife Area are located around Keith Sebelius Reservoir. The reservoir is an impoundment of Prairie Dog Creek, which flows through the rolling mixedgrass prairie of the High Plains. Drive south of the park office and over the railroad gorge to reach the sizable prairie dog town. The black-tailed prairie dog, named for its black-tipped tail and dog-like bark, uses mounds as sentinel stations from which to watch for predators such as coyotes, prairie falcons, golden eagles, and badgers. When the burrows are no longer used by the prairie dogs they are taken over by other animals including black widow spiders, ornate box turtles, bull snakes, and the comical burrowing owl. If you drive along the lake roads during migrations you can expect to see a great variety of waterfowl and shorebirds. On occasion, a migrant osprey can be spotted fishing the waters. Ring-necked pheasants are abundant in the surrounding wildlife area, as are deer and wild turkeys. In early summer, reptiles, including six-lined racerunners, western hognose snakes, and plains garter snakes, can be found around the rocky ridges and open grasslands of the range management area.

Directions: To reach Prairie Dog State Park, travel 4 miles west of Norton on U.S. 36, then 1 mile south. Pick up your park permit, maps, and information on prairie dogs at the park office. **Ownership:** KDWP (913-877-2953) **7,850 acres** P ♔♙ H₂0 ⊼ Ⓐ ⊜ ⇒

One of our most fascinating wildlife species to watch, black-tailed prairie dogs live in "towns" and depend on a complicated system of "barks" to communicate. The all-clear signal consists of a jubilant bark while standing on their hind legs, head back, and front legs reaching for the sky.

Bob Gress

86 Antelope Lake

Don't expect to see antelope in this area. The name comes from Antelope Creek, which flows into the lake. The flooded timber creates great habitat for wood ducks. Careful observers should find them. Also be alert for beavers and muskrats, sometimes seen at the wooded west end of the lake. Western painted turtles often sun themselves on partially submerged logs. Both mule deer and white-tailed deer sometimes graze in adjacent fields. During migrations the area is a stopping spot for several species of ducks, mergansers, grebes, and coots. The wooded areas around the lake attract a variety of woodpeckers and songbirds. Great blue herons and belted kingfishers are usually seen along the shoreline. While in the area visit Sheridan State Fishing Lake as well. Many of the same wildlife species are found at Sheridan, but different terrain—rocky outcroppings and sparse vegetation—provides ideal habitat for several species of snakes and lizards.

Directions: Antelope Lake is 14.5 miles west and 1 mile north of Hill City on U.S. 24. Sheridan State Fishing Lake is located 7 miles west of Antelope Lake or 11 miles east and 1 mile north of Hoxie on U.S. 24. **Ownership:** Graham County (913-674-3453) **106 acres** ▢ 👫 ⊼ ◎ 🛥

87 Arikaree Breaks Wildlife Drive

This scenic drive through the far northwestern corner of Kansas takes travelers into the unique "badlands" near the Arikaree River and gives them a view of the eroded breaks. The scenic road (which may not be passable if muddy) travels up and over the rock formation locally known as Devil's Cap. Only 3 miles of the Arikaree River are within the state's borders; the river runs from Colorado, across the extreme corner of Kansas, and into Nebraska. Here the shortgrass prairie is dotted with yucca and prickly pear cactus. Tracks of mule deer and coyote are frequently seen in the sand along the roads. Lesser earless lizards are also common in these sandy areas. The most common birds are horned larks, vesper sparrows, western meadowlarks, mourning doves, and American kestrels. Rock wrens are found along the rocky outcroppings of Devil's Cap. Small mammals found in the area include thirteen-lined ground squirrels and Ord's kangaroo rats. Watch for their diggings along the roadways. A black-tailed prairie dog town, complete with a few burrowing owls, can also be seen along the drive. The owls usually stand at the burrow entrances or perch on fence posts. An interesting side trip, which may present opportunities to see deer, turkeys, and other wildlife, starts along a county road next to the Republican River just west of St. Francis. Go either upriver or downriver.

Directions: From U.S. 36, 2 miles west of St. Francis, travel north 17.5 miles on K-27 to an intersection that is 4 miles south of the Nebraska border and 1.2 miles north of the Williams Natural Gas pump station. From this intersection go 2 miles west and turn north. A 16-mile loop drive begins from this intersection. Travel north 1.2 miles to the prairie dog town (which is on private property, so view it from the road). Continue north, turning left at every road intersection. The most scenic breaks are about 2.5 miles past the Arikaree River valley. **Ownership:** Private

88 Mount Sunflower

It's not exactly the Alps but it is the highest point in Kansas! Mount Sunflower, 0.5 miles east of the Colorado border in Wallace County, has an elevation of 4,039 feet and consists of a gently sloping hill of shortgrass prairie. Fun-loving visitors fill the register with comments typical of mountain-climbing adventurers. Many species of western wildlife are found in the surrounding grassland. Pronghorns are here as well as south of U.S. 40 between Sharon Springs and the Colorado border and on K-27 north from Sharon Springs to the Sherman County line. Mule deer, coyotes, black-tailed jackrabbits, and swift fox all live in the surrounding prairie. Early morning and late evening are the best times to watch for them. Along the sand roadways are many burrows of both nocturnal (active at night) Ord's kangaroo rats and diurnal (active in the day) thirteen-lined ground squirrels. Ground squirrels are also common on Mount Sunflower itself. The most visible birds in the area include horned larks and lapland longspurs during winter and early spring. During summer, vesper sparrows, Cassin's sparrows, and western meadowlarks are found. You may also spot ferruginous, Swainson's, and red-tailed hawks and, if you're lucky, golden eagles. If you are here in the spring, take a side excursion to the old Sherman County State Fishing Lake, now dry. There are excellent viewing opportunities for deer fawns on late May and early June evenings.

Directions: From Sharon Springs travel 15.5 miles west on U.S. 40 to an intersection with a gravel road. Follow signs to Mount Sunflower, 11 miles north and 1 mile west. Sherman County State Fishing Lake lies along the Smoky Hill River, 8 miles south and 3 miles west of Goodland. **Ownership:** Private **P**

Mike Blair

When Coronado entered the area of what is now Kansas in 1541, pronghorns (antelope) were as numerous as bison.

89 Scott State Park

Scott State Park, the first state park in Kansas, lies along Lake Scott in picturesque Ladder Creek Canyon. The oasis-like setting is very popular with campers and anglers. El Cuartelejo, the only known Indian pueblo in Kansas, was established in the 1600s by Taos Indians and later occupied by Picuris Indians. Both groups were attracted to the area by the many large springs, one of which (Big Springs) can be reached by hiking on a short nature trail. This spring, which provides a flow of about 400 gallons per minute of 58° water, has been stocked with rainbow trout. The area's unique wildlife species—the Scott riffle beetle—is a tiny, seldom-seen insect that lives in the springs feeding into the lake. Because this beetle is found nowhere else in the world, it has been listed as a Kansas endangered species. White-tailed deer are common in the area and mule deer are occasionally seen. Beaver dams are seen along Ladder Creek. Perhaps the most visible species of wildlife are the thirteen-lined ground squirrels, wild turkeys, black-billed magpies, and turkey vultures. Early in the morning the vultures are commonly seen roosting on the bluffs or perched in cottonwood trees or on fence posts. They wait for the warming air to create thermals capable of maintaining their effortless soaring. The area is also attractive to other interesting birds: Lazuli buntings, Say's phoebes, common poorwills, and black headed grosbeaks. During summer nesting rock wrens scurry along the canyon walls. The area is also one of the most predictable places in Kansas to find nesting yellow-breasted chats. At the south end of the park is a managed herd of elk and bison. The elk are often difficult to see. If the bison are not visible, take the first road south of the pens to the top of the surrounding hills. They are often seen grazing on the upper pasture. Reptile lovers should note that this site is known for its large variety and numbers.

Directions: From Scott City, Scott State Park can be reached by traveling 10 miles north on U.S. 83 to the junction of K-95. The park entrance is on K-95, another 3 miles north. **Ownership:** KDWP (316-872-2061) **1,120 acres**

P 👫 H₂0 ⊼ Ⓐ 🚶 🚣

Mike Blair

While looking forward to its upcoming meal of thirteen-lined ground squirrel, this swift fox stops to watch the intruder. This smallest canid of Kansas occurs only in the western third of the state.

90 Chalk Pyramids

Although dry here in recent years, the Smoky Hill River once had enough flow to carve unique "badlands" in the fossil-rich chalk layers of western Kansas. One of the best-known formations is the area known as the Chalk Pyramids, sometimes referred to as Monument Rocks. In addition to the unusual geology, the area also offers some interesting habitat for wildlife. Small holes in the formations provide nesting cavities for our smallest falcon, the American kestrel. Pigeons also fly from ledge to ledge as they commonly do in most cities. Here we gain an understanding of this introduced bird's natural habitat in Europe and why they are also called rock doves. Pronghorns inhabit the surrounding shortgrass prairie. Although they are large mammals, their colors make them surprisingly difficult to see. Also in the area are coyotes, black-tailed jackrabbits, lesser earless lizards, and the venomous western rattlesnake. Birders find Cassin's sparrows, ferruginous hawks, and golden eagles of special interest. Common birds include horned larks, vesper sparrows, western meadowlarks, and black-billed magpies. Winter brings prairie falcons, rough-legged hawks, and large flocks of lapland longspurs. For further exploration of this region, acquire maps of Logan, Gove, and Trego counties and try the back roads that criss-cross the river. There are few good east-west drives, and many of these roads are impassable when wet! Sharks' teeth and other fossils are exposed after rains erode the gravel and rocks. Visit the fossil displays in the Sternberg Museum at Fort Hays State University in Hays and the Fick Fossil Museum in Oakley.

Directions: Smoky Hill River crosses U.S. 83 about 25 miles north of Scott City. North of the river 2.5 miles a sign directs visitors another 4 miles east and 2 miles south to the Chalk Pyramids. **Ownership:** Private **10 acres** **P**

The Chalk Pyramids are part of the "badlands" along the Smoky Hill River in western Kansas. These eroded chalk formations are famous worldwide for producing hundreds of species of fossils.

Bob Gress

91 Castle Rock Drive

This drive of nearly 40 miles will take you south on Castle Rock Road from I-70 at Quinter, east to the Castle Rock outcrop, and back north on Banner Road to I-70 at Collyer. These roads can be hazardous when muddy, so use good judgment. As you drive over this rolling country you will pass through croplands, fallow fields, and pastures. Several stream channels with riparian vegetation and desolate chalk canyons are on the route. Watch for pronghorns, mule deer, white-tailed deer, and black-tailed jackrabbits. In summer, survey the canyons and roads for black-billed magpies, rock wrens, mourning doves, loggerhead shrikes, vesper sparrows, and lark sparrows. At night, Ord's kangaroo rats are often seen crossing the roads. Late fall through early spring, horned larks, longspurs, rough-legged hawks, prairie falcons, and northern harriers are frequently observed. Northern shrikes are occasionally sighted. Coyotes, red-tailed hawks, American kestrels, ferruginous hawks, and meadowlarks are seen throughout the year. Some prairie dog towns are found in heavily grazed areas. They are inhabited not only by black-tailed prairie dogs but also by burrowing owls and thirteen-lined ground squirrels. When you cross the cattle grate to enter the Castle Rock area, notice the ungrazed area ahead. Follow the road to the right and into Hackberry Creek Valley. The large single chalk outcrop is Castle Rock. The flat grassy area is chalk flat prairie, dominated by little bluestem, sideoats grama, and saltgrass. Many wildflowers bloom from late spring to early fall. Look for ruts left by Butterfield stagecoaches that passed just north of the rock in 1865. Lesser earless lizards, ornate box turtles, plains garter snakes, and western hognose snakes are found in the area. The presence of western rattlesnakes adds an extra titillation to this trip. Watch for great horned owls that nest in the chalk bluffs to the south. Look for sharks' teeth and other fossils among the chalk rocks and gravel. This area was once the bottom of a large ocean.

Directions: From I-70 take the Quinter Exit (107) south on Castle Rock Road for 14.6 miles. Turn east and go 4 miles to the Castle Rock outcrop turnoff. Drive 1 mile north to the cattle grate. Follow the road to the right and circle into Hackberry Creek valley and back to the grate (a little over 2 miles). This is private land, so please treat it with respect. Return south 1 mile to the road. Travel east 2.8 miles to Banner Road. Take Banner Road 12.4 miles north to I-70 at Collyer. **Ownership:** Private

92 Cedar Bluff Reservoir

Don't let the receding water level of Cedar Bluff Reservoir dampen your impression of this premier wildlife area. Although boat ramps have been left high and dry amid groves of lake-bottom cottonwoods, there is still enough water to attract a variety of water birds. During fall and spring migrations, the lake is home to many kinds of ducks, geese, and shorebirds. Throughout the winter, Canada geese are seen on the former fish hatchery ponds located below the dam. Winter also draws bald eagles to Cedar Bluff. Look for them from the road across the dam. During summer, hawks and turkey vultures soar effortlessly for hours on thermals created by the dam. A good viewing spot is the hilltop adjoining the south end of the dam. A little farther west, enjoy a panoramic view from the tall limestone bluffs on the south shore. Campers are often serenaded by yapping coyotes in the night. A visit to Cedar Bluff should include a driving tour of the Cedar Bluff Wildlife Area at the western end of the reservoir. If muddy, the roads may be impassable without 4-wheel drive. Wildlife sightings can include both mule deer and white-tailed deer. Also watch for eastern cottontails, black-tailed jackrabbits, and the large stick nests of the eastern wood rats. Summer birds include black-billed magpies, rock wrens, and Bell's vireos. During winter, hawks take advantage of the rodent populations in the surrounding prairie. Watch for red-tailed hawks, ferruginous hawks, northern harriers, prairie falcons, and American kestrels. At dusk watch for long-eared owls and the moth-like flight of short-eared owls as they swoop low over the prairie searching for prey. Wild turkeys are often seen. Check chalk outcrops and gravel areas around the reservoir for fossils.

Directions: To reach Cedar Bluff Reservoir, travel 13.1 miles south of I-70 on K-147 to the turnoff to the main office and campground. If you're visiting Cedar Bluff Wildlife Area, be sure to pick up a map at the office. The best parts of the wildlife area are on the southwest side of the lake. **Ownership:** USBuRec (913-726-4745); KDWP (913-726-3212) **17,600 acres**

🅿 👫 H₂0 🌳 ⓐ 🚶 🚶‍♀️ 🚂

Southwest

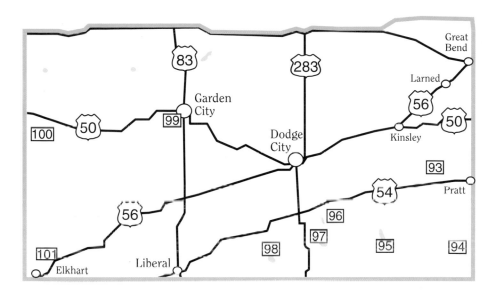

93 Pratt Sand Hills and Texas Lake Wildlife Areas

Pratt Sand Hills Wildlife Area, a unique sand prairie habitat, is probably best known as the easternmost range of lesser prairie chickens in Kansas. The best time to view the birds is from late March through early May when they gather early in the morning on their booming grounds, or leks, to display. These areas may change from year to year. Drive out before sunrise, shut off the engine, and listen carefully! The area also has a large population of kangaroo rats and predators that depend on them. Watch for badgers, coyotes, and Swainson's hawks. Wild turkeys, black-billed magpies, loggerhead shrikes, and Mississippi kites may also be found. Reptiles include prairie lizards and six-lined racerunners. The sandy roads leading into this area may be impassable at certain times of the year. During dry weather the sand may be so deep that typical automobiles drag and get stuck. At the Texas Lake Wildlife Area, several small lakes and marshy sloughs attract waterfowl, shorebirds, and other wetland species.

Directions: To reach Texas Lake from Cullison, go 4.4 miles west on U.S. 54 to the sign directing visitors 2.5 miles north. To reach Pratt Sandhills Wildlife Area from Texas Lake Wildlife Area, travel 1 mile west of Texas Lake and 6.5 miles north. **Ownership:** KDWP (316-672-5911) **5,797 acres** **P**

Bob Gress

With their nocturnal habits and camouflage fur, bobcats are ideally suited to life as predators. Although fairly common in Kansas, the bobcat is rarely seen.

94 Gypsum Hills Scenic Drive

One of the best-kept secrets in Kansas is the Gypsum Hills, sometimes called Red Hills. The rolling hills, buttes, and mesas are graced with a generous supply of wildflowers. Red cedar trees dot the landscape. They, along with little bluestem and sideoats grama grasses, make this one of the most scenic areas in the Midwest. The small blue fruits of the cedars provide food for one of the state's more unexpected wildlife species. During the winter months, flocks of mountain bluebirds are hundreds of miles from their usual haunts. They perch on roadside fences, hover over the prairie, and feed in the cedars. The cedars also attract wintering American robins, cedar waxwings, and Townsend's solitaires. While driving the roads of Barber County be alert for armadillos, wild turkeys, deer, roadrunners, black-tailed prairie dogs, and elusive bobcats and coyotes. Under many of the area's bridges, cliff swallows build large colonies of gourd-shaped mud nests. Of special interest are the Texas horned lizards, collared lizards, western rattlesnakes, and tarantulas sometimes found by observant travelers.

Directions: Gypsum Hills Scenic Drive is a marked 20-mile loop, beginning 3.5 miles west of Medicine Lodge on U.S. 160. If roads are dry, another interesting drive begins in Hardtner. Go west out of town on the paved country road. In 11.1 miles, check under the bridge over the Salt Fork of the Arkansas River for thousands of cliff swallow nests. Continue turning right at all intersections, and 24.4 miles from Hardtner you will find a few buildings marking the remnants of Aetna. Continue north and at 32.2 miles you encounter a large prairie dog town. Look carefully for burrowing owls! You will find the town of Deerhead (just one building) at 36.7 miles and U.S. 160 at 39.7 miles. To explore further take U.S. 160 west 1.2 miles and travel north to Sun City. This is a great spot to enjoy a Kansas sunset! In the evening twilight, watch for bats fluttering overhead near streams as they emerge from the many hidden caves in the hills. **Ownership:** Private

95 Lake Coldwater

This spring-fed lake is a source of pride to area residents. A 3.8-mile road circles the lake and offers good visibility to the entire lake surface. During the winter, the lake attracts Canada geese, mallards, common mergansers, goldeneyes, pintails, gadwalls, and most other common ducks. During migrations white pelicans sometimes use the lake as a stopover. Ospreys are common in fall and bald eagles often winter in the area. At both ends of the lake, beaver activity is visible on the streambank trees. Several beaver dams and ponds are also present. Deer are commonly seen near the locust grove below the dam. Other area mammals include muskrats, raccoons, cottontails, and thirteen-lined ground squirrels. The lake's well-maintained grounds are ideal for robins, western kingbirds, and northern orioles. The grassy areas are inhabited by grasshopper sparrows, western meadowlarks, and prairie lizards.

Directions: Lake Coldwater is located 0.5 miles south and 0.5 miles west of the city of Coldwater. **Ownership:** City of Coldwater (316-582-2940) **930 acres**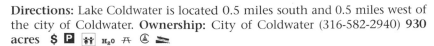

96 Clark State Fishing Lake

Approaching through flat farmlands and pasturelands, visitors are pleasantly surprised to discover Clark State Fishing Lake nestled in the deep Bluff Creek canyon. Several short drives or walks, on both sides of the lake, provide scenic vistas of this rugged western Kansas treasure. The mixedgrass prairie hilltops and canyon sides are dominated by yucca and aromatic sumac. Burrows of kangaroo rats are seen under the yucca clumps and along the roadside soil banks. You may spot coyote tracks in the dust; watch for these wily predators in early morning and late evening. Interesting reptiles include collared and Texas horned lizards and western rattlesnakes. Lark sparrows are found along the roads, and rock wrens find suitable nesting habitat along the steep canyon walls. At the far northeast corner of the lake is the Jay R. Wood Memorial Nature Trail, which follows Bluff Creek through tall cottonwood bottomlands. Red-headed woodpeckers, white-breasted nuthatches, and other woodland birds are found along the trail. The lake is attractive to ducks and geese, and ospreys are common during the fall migration. Herons, gulls, and terns are also seen. During summer, both eastern and western kingbirds nest in the campground trees and noisily defend their territories.

Directions: From Kingsdown, follow K-94 south 10 miles. The highway ends at the lake. **Ownership:** KDWP (316-873-2572) **1,240 acres**

97 Big Basin and St. Jacob's Well

By following U.S. Highway 283 for 1.4 miles you can experience the floor of Big Basin, which most likely resulted from salts dissolving several hundred feet below the earth's surface. In Little Basin, about 0.5 miles to the east, is a spring known as St. Jacob's Well. From a distance, the spot appears to be an oasis of cottonwood trees. Tracks indicate the value of permanent water to the wildlife of the area. This site preserves some mixedgrass prairie that is rich with wildflowers during spring. Western meadowlarks and grasshopper sparrows are common during the nesting period. Collared lizards and six-lined racerunners sun on exposed rocks. The most visible animals of the area are bison, which dot the distant hillsides or sometimes roll in the dust in the middle of the access road. These animals can be unpredictable; stay in your vehicle if they are close. Many bison wear identification tags in their ears.

Directions: From Minneola travel 12 miles south on U.S. 283 to the intersection of U.S. 160. Continue south from this intersection, following both highways 3.2 miles to a roadside information sign describing Big Basin and the bison. Continue south another 0.6 miles to the entrance gate on the east side of the road. It is 1.7 miles from the highway to St. Jacob's Well. **Ownership:** KDWP (316-873-2572) **1,800 acres** P

98 Meade State Park and Fishing Lake

In addition to a scenic fishing lake and well-developed campground, Meade State Park and Fishing Lake offers much to wildlife watchers. Birders regularly turn up unusual sightings at the area, including the brown pelican and magnificent frigatebird. These apparently lost birds seem to be attracted to the oasis-like habitat of woods and water in an area dominated by flat, open farmland. Nesting Mississippi kites, red-headed woodpeckers, northern orioles, and western kingbirds are at home among park users, who often camp and picnic under tall cottonwoods. The large cattail marsh is alive in the evenings with swarms of red-winged blackbirds and barn swallows. During winter the lake attracts flocks of ducks and geese. The cedar trees on the north side of the lake also attract eastern bluebirds, robins, cedar waxwings, and Townsend's solitaires. At the picnic area adjacent to Meade Fish Hatchery a tapped artesian well provides spring water to a narrow stream partly overgrown by watercress. This spring is inhabited by the Arkansas darter—a small fish that lives in the watercress in spring-fed streams in the region and is threatened in Kansas. An interpretive sign identifies the area. White-tailed deer are frequently seen in the woods around the fish hatchery and along the hiking trail around the west side of the lake.

Directions: From the intersection of U.S. 160 in Meade, travel 13.7 miles south on K-23 to the state park entrance. To visit Meade Fish Hatchery, continue west from the entrance, turning right at the next two corners. Ownership: KDWP (316-873-2572) 923 acres ▣ ⚐ H₂0 ⚞ Ⓐ ⚐ ⚓ ⊛

99 Finney Game Refuge

This refuge, managed primarily for its herd of more than 100 bison, is divided into three large pastures. For safety the public is not allowed in the areas containing the bison. Access is limited, and prior arrangements need to be made for a refuge tour. Notices on the information signs at the office and parking lots explain which pastures are open to the public as the bison herd is seasonally moved. The north sandpit area is always open to the public. The sandsage prairie habitat attracts an interesting collection of wildlife species. Mule deer and coyotes are sometimes seen. The area also supports a small colony of black-tailed prairie dogs. The diggings of Ord's kangaroo rats are found throughout the area. Nesting birds include lesser prairie chickens, lark sparrows, Cassin's sparrows, and western meadowlarks. You may also wish to visit Lee Richardson Zoo, which is less than a mile from the refuge. In addition to the confined animals, wildlife watchers will find nesting house finches and Mississippi kites in summer, and in winter the duck pond attracts large flocks of migrating waterfowl.

Directions: Finney Game Refuge is located 1 mile south of Garden City on Business U.S. 83. Lee Richardson Zoo is located less than 1 mile north of the refuge just inside the city limits. Ownership: KDWP (316-872-2061) 3,800 acres ▣

100 Syracuse River Road

This 19-mile drive connects the towns of Syracuse and Coolidge, just 2 miles from the Colorado state line. The road runs along the south side of the Arkansas River. To the south lie rolling sand dunes covered with sagebrush, yucca, and grasses. The most visible species of wildlife along the drive is the colorful black-billed magpie. At times, 20 or more can be seen foraging together or flying in loose flocks. Look for their large stick nests, often 3 feet in diameter. Along the river road, visitors encounter large, picturesque stands of stately cottonwoods that provide nesting cavities for red-headed woodpeckers, northern flickers, and American kestrels. The wooded river bottoms also provide good habitat for mule deer, white-tailed deer, wild turkeys, and coyotes. This is one of the few places in the state where porcupines occur. Watch for them feeding in the cottonwood trees—from a distance a porcupine looks very much like a squirrel nest. The sand dunes support lesser prairie chickens and scaled quail. While in the region, visit Hamilton Wildlife Area. The dry lake bed is a stark reminder of a dwindling water supply. A spring at the north end of the area has several dams constructed by land-locked beaver. The many rodent holes on the edges of the sandy roads are created by Ord's kangaroo rats and thirteen-lined ground squirrels. Their presence explains the coyote tracks in the sand!

Directions: From Syracuse the river road is located 1.4 miles south of U.S. 50 on K-27. Follow the river road west 17.6 miles to the town of Coolidge. Note: Several black-tailed prairie dog towns can be reached by traveling east on the river road. Hamilton County Wildlife Area is 3.2 miles west and 2.2 miles north of Syracuse. **Ownership:** Private

Mike Blair

The mule deer feeds mainly on tree twigs and shrubs and sometimes on grasses and wildflowers. Common in the Cimarron, Smoky Hill and Solomon river valleys, the "muley" differs from the "white-tail" by having large ears, a short white tail with a black tip, and antlers with Y-shaped forks.

101 Cimarron National Grasslands

Cimarron National Grasslands is well known to wildlife enthusiasts who travel to Morton County to explore the rolling sandsage prairie. Sand sagebrush is a conspicuous 3-foot-tall shrub with gray-green foliage. Local wildflowers include silky prairie clover, sweet sand verbena, sand milkweed, hairy gaura, field goosefoot, and wild begonia. Elk and pronghorns are found in the area. If you wish to see them, call the district office for the current location of the herds. While driving the roads be alert for porcupines. Bird species normally associated with the arid southwest or the mountains are sometimes found here. Throughout the year birders search for rarities such as mountain chickadees, scrub jays, Steller's jays, roadrunners, bushtits, curve-billed thrashers, and western tanagers. During early August, mountain plovers are sometimes found. Nesting birds include Cassin's sparrows, lark buntings, scaled quail, and lesser prairie chickens. Several prairie chicken booming grounds, or leks, have observation blinds for public use. Call the district office to make reservations. Several species of amphibians are commonly found on the grasslands. After rains in spring and summer, drive the roads at night and listen for the calls of plains spadefoot toads, Great Plains toads, Woodhouse's toads, and plains leopard frogs. Common reptiles include ornate box turtles, northern earless lizards, Texas horned lizards, and western rattlesnakes. The self-guided auto tour is a scenic 50-mile drive that highlights many of the interesting wildlife features, including a prairie dog town. Portions of the historic Santa Fe Trail, marked by limestone posts, are visible in many locations. One stop is Point of Rocks, an important landmark on the trail and a great place to find rock wrens. Middle Spring provided trail travelers with a dependable, year-round source of water. Today, pools of water are dammed by beaver. The water and trees are an attractive oasis to wildlife of all kinds.

Directions: The District Office, identified as the Cimarron National Grasslands Range Station, is on U.S. 56 in Elkhart. Stop here (hours: M–F, 8–5) to pick up a map, wildlife checklist, and the self-guided auto tour booklet; or write for the material: Cimarron National Grasslands, 242 Highway 56 East, PO Box J, Elkhart KS 67950. The self-guided auto tour begins 2 miles north of Elkhart on K-27. There is a picnic area south of the river 7.5 miles north of Elkhart on K-27. South of the picnic area is a road east to a campground. Middle Spring and Point of Rocks are reached from K-27 by turning west, 0.5 miles north of the Cimarron River bridge. **Ownership:** U.S.D.A. Forest Service (316-697-4621) **108,175 acres** P ♯♯ H₂0 ⊼ Ⓛ ♯♯

Field Guide and References

Mammals

Bee, James W., Gregory Glass, Robert S. Hoffmann, and Robert R.
Patterson. *Mammals in Kansas*. Lawrence: University of Kansas
Museum of Natural History, 1981.
Burt, William H. *A Field Guide to the Mammals*. 3d ed. Peterson Field Guide
Series. Boston: Houghton Mifflin, 1976.
Murie, Olaus. *A Field Guide to Animal Tracks*. 2d ed. Peterson Field Guide
Series. Boston: Houghton Mifflin, 1975.

Birds

Scott, Shirley L., ed. *Field Guide to the Birds of North America*. 2d ed.
Washington, D.C.: National Geographic Society, 1983.
Peterson, Roger Tory. *A Field Guide to Eastern Birds: A Field Guide to the
Birds East of the Rockies*. Peterson Field Guide Series. Boston:
Houghton Mifflin, 1984.
Robbins, Chandler S., et al. *Birds of North America*. Golden Field Guide
Series. Golden Press, 1983.
Thompson, Max C., and Charles Ely. *Birds in Kansas*. 2 vols. Lawrence:
University Press of Kansas, vol. 1, 1989; vol. 2, 1992.
Zimmerman, John. *The Birds of Konza: The Avian Ecology of the Tallgrass
Prairie*. Lawrence: University Press of Kansas, 1993.
Zimmerman, John T., and Sebastian T. Patti. *A Guide to Bird Finding in
Kansas and Western Missouri*. Lawrence: University Press of Kansas,
1988.

Amphibians and Reptiles

Caldwell, Janalee, and Joseph Collins. *Turtles in Kansas*. Lawrence:
University of Kansas Museum of Natural History, 1981.
Collins, Joseph T. *Amphibians and Reptiles in Kansas*. 3d ed. Lawrence:
University of Kansas Museum of Natural History, 1993.
Collins, Joseph T., and Suzanne L. Collins. *Reptiles and Amphibians of the
Cimarron National Grasslands*. Morton County, Kans.: United States
Forest Service, 1991.
Conant, Roger, and Joseph Collins. *A Field Guide to Reptiles and
Amphibians: Eastern and Central North America*. Peterson Field Guide
Series. Boston: Houghton Mifflin, 1975.

Fish

Cross, Frank, and Joseph Collins. *Fishes in Kansas*. Lawrence: University of
Kansas Museum of Natural History, 1975.
Tomelleri, Joseph R., and Mark E. Eberle. *Fishes of the Central United States*.
Lawrence: University Press of Kansas, 1990.

Insects

Borror, Donald J., and Richard E. White. *A Field Guide to the Insects of America North of Mexico*. Peterson Field Guide Series. Boston: Houghton Mifflin, 1970.

Ely, Charles A., Marvin D. Schwilling, and Marvin E. Rolfs. *An Annotated List of the Butterflies of Kansas*. Fort Hays, Kans.: Fort Hays State University, 1986.

Heitzman, Richard, and Joan Heitzman. *Butterflies and Moths of Missouri*. Missouri Department of Conservation, 1987.

Schwilling, Marvin D., and Charles A. Ely. *Kansas School Naturalist Checklist of Kansas Butterflies*. Emporia, Kans.: Emporia State University, 1991.

Plants

Bare, Janét. *Wildflowers and Weeds of Kansas*. Lawrence: University Press of Kansas, 1979.

Barkley, T. M. *Field Guide to the Common Weeds of Kansas*. Lawrence: University Press of Kansas, 1983.

Freeman, Craig C., and Eileen K. Schofield. *Roadside Wildflowers of the Southern Great Plains*. Lawrence: University Press of Kansas, 1991.

Kindscher, Kelly. *Edible Wild Plants of the Prairie: An Ethnobotanical Guide*. Lawrence: University Press of Kansas, 1987.

———. *Medicinal Wild Plants of the Prairie: An Ethnobotanical Guide*. Lawrence: University Press of Kansas, 1992.

Ohlenbusch, Paul D., Elizabeth P. Hodges, and Susan Pope. *Range Grasses of Kansas*. Kansas Cooperative Extension Services, July 1983. Publication C-567.

Owensby, Clenton. *Kansas Prairie Wildflowers*. Ames: Iowa State University Press, 1980.

Stephens, H. A. *Trees, Shrubs, and Woody Vines in Kansas*. Lawrence: University Press of Kansas, 1969.

Geology

Buchanan, Rex, ed. *Kansas Geology: An Introduction to Landscape, Rocks, Minerals, and Fossils*. Lawrence: University Press of Kansas, 1984.

Muilenburg, Grace, and Ada Swineford. *Land of the Post Rock: Its Origins, History, and People*. Lawrence: University Press of Kansas, 1975.

Wilson, Frank. *Kansas Landscapes: A Geologic Diary*. Lawrence: Kansas Geological Survey, Educational Series 5, 1978.

Travel

Buchanan, Rex, and James R. McCauley. *Roadside Kansas: A Traveler's Guide to Its Geology and Landmarks*. Lawrence: University Press of Kansas, 1987.

Harper, Steve. *83,000 Square Miles: No Lines, No Waiting*. Wichita: Wichita Eagle and Beacon Publishing, 1990.

Penner, Mil, and Carol Schmidt. *Kansas Journeys*. Inman, Kans.: Sounds of Kansas, 1985.

Penner, Mil, and Marci Penner. *Kansas Weekend Guide*. Inman, Kans.: Sounds of Kansas, 1990.

Shortridge, James R. *Kaw Valley Landscapes: A Traveler's Guide to Northeastern Kansas*. Lawrence: University Press of Kansas, 1988.

General

Collins, Joseph T., Bob Gress, Gerald Wiens, and Suzanne L. Collins. *Kansas Wildlife*. Lawrence: University Press of Kansas, 1991.

Collins, Joseph T., ed. *Natural Kansas*. Lawrence: University Press of Kansas, 1985.

Potts, George D., and Joseph T. Collins. *A Checklist of the Vertebrate Animals of Kansas*. Lawrence: University of Kansas Museum of Natural History, 1991.

Reichman, O. J. *Konza Prairie: A Tallgrass Natural History*. Lawrence: University Press of Kansas, 1987.

Zimmerman, John. *Cheyenne Bottoms: Wetland in Jeopardy*. Lawrence: University Press of Kansas, 1990.